St. George's - a Wat

An illustrated history of St.George's Church, Kidderminster, together with its schools and daughter churches during the period 1818 - 2008.

Written and compiled by

Melvyn Thompson

St.George's - a Waterloo Church   ISBN 0 9535442 2 2

Published by the Hencroft Press   September 2009

All rights reserved. No part of this book may be reproduced or transmitted in any form or by any means, electronic or mechanical, including photocopying, recording or by any information storage or retrieval system, without the permission of the author, or his representatives, in writing.

Profit from the sale of this book goes to St.George's Church Restoration fund

All enquires to the author -
Melvyn Thompson, 2 Flint Close, Kidderminster DY10 1YF
Telephone number 01562 67077
or St.George's Parish Office 01562 822131   www.stgeorgeskidderminster.co.uk

Printed by
Stargold Ltd. Digital House, Stourport Road, Kidderminster

Cover pictures -

Outer front :	St.George's through the trees from St.Mary's Tower.	*Amanda Hall*
Inner front :	Views of the church from Coventry Street	*Author' s Collection*
Outer rear :	Collage of photographs taken at Harvest 2007	*Author' s Collection*
Inner rear :	Collage of general photographs 2008	*Author' s Collection*
	United Parish Service 2007	*Mattie Underhill*

Background

My regular attendance at St.George's started in 1944 when, as a seven-year-old treble, I joined the choir. Before that date I was an occasional visitor with my parents who, I recall, brought paper and pencil to keep me quiet during the service!

The Church became part of my life and I started to keep the service sheets, old parish magazines and photographs as they became available. Over the years the collection grew and in more recent times others, knowing my interest in history, have passed on more memorabilia. When the Rev. Canon Nick Barker was clearing out the rectory, before his move to Durham in 2007, he took the opportunity to add even more to the collection.

Someone remarked "you've got enough to write a book" and so I decided to do just that. Basic research started and it soon became apparent that others had little boxes of history just like mine. With their help and information gleaned from four published works the outline of the jigsaw was on the table. However, the larger pieces came as a result of the hours spent at the County Records Office, Kidderminster Library, the Parish Office and at home searching through the ageing registers and minute books.

In the writing of this book there have been three main concerns. Firstly, with so much information available it is inevitable that some important sections may have been overlooked or misinterpreted. Secondly, and perhaps the biggest concern was who to mention [or not] by name. Finally, having witnessed over sixty years of church life from the choir stalls it may appear that there is a bias in that direction.

I can only say I have done my best to strike a fair balance on these important issues.

St.George's Church has a fascinating history and I sincerely hope you enjoy reading about it as much as I have writing about it.

Melvyn Thompson
October 2008

The photograph above was taken in the late 1940s by Leonard Brooks at his studio on Station Hill. The studio has a link with the St.George's story because it was there that William Thompson [no relation] developed many of the original photographs copied in this book.

I went to the studio, by appointment, with my father. I recall that my black cassock was very old and probably dated back to 1927. In those days we had to provide our own Eton collars and bow ties. The surplices were well darned and regularly washed and starched at the Kidderminster Steam Laundry - my mother was dismayed at the creases highlighted by the camera. I also recall that when I arrived at the studio I had forgotten my hymnbook and so Mr Brooks' Oxford Dictionary provided a perfect substitute.

Acknowledgements

I am indebted to the following -
The late Ken Tomkinson and George Hall for "Kidderminster since 1800".
The diarist and former churchwarden William Whitcomb [1866-1960].
Don Gilbert's record of Transactions for Worcestershire Archaeological Society 2000 - "William Knight, a Worcestershire Architect".
Michael Hale's book "Hassocks & Cassocks - Inkwells & School Bells" - an excellent companion telling more about many characters mentioned in this book.
Mattie Underhill's 2006 booklet about St.Chad's Church entitled "50 Years on Comberton".
Mattie also made available her excellent collection of church photographs.

It was good to make contact with former incumbents particularly the Revs. Edward Montague-Youens, Peter Chippendale, John Ilson, Nick Barker and Andi Jones. I thank them for photographs and their help and enthusiasm for the project. I would also like to thank the Rev. Hugh Burton for his help, support and permission to reproduce the vestry photographs and other church information.

A number of others have also provided information from their store of parish knowledge namely -
Tim Morris, Norman Tatlow, Rosemarie Moore, Michael Linegar, Keith Mullard, Peggy and Catherine Guest together with information collected by the Rev. Leslie Guest. Architect David Mills of Hagley. Gwen Gwillam provided much of the information about St.George's School and much more from her memory store. Gordon Higgs for his information about the donations and artifacts. Steve and Janet at the Parish Office who also helped organise a Latin translation by Fr. Guy of the Oratory, Birmingham.
Tony Woodward and John Clarke for help with dates and non-confidential financial information. Phillip Dullforce and a number of others who have passed on snippets of information so important to the story.
Malcolm Upsall provided information and photographs about St.Cecilia's and Stewart Manser with his information about St.George's Club.

My friends in the various historical groups have also passed on information and photographs. Chris Pickford "told" me about the bells; Bob Millward, a former boy chorister; Jeff Lane; Goff Jones who provided some original photographs including his collection of church "Lustreware". Nigel Gilbert and Nicky Griffiths of the Kidderminster Historical Project.
While the majority of photographs were from my own collection, others were supplied by Amanda Hall, David Mills, Robert Barber, Richard Warner, Eddie Curry and Kidderminster Library.
Sketches by Ken Jackson, Roger Sullivan and Muriel Robinson.

I would also like to thank the staff at the County Records Office and Kidderminster Public Library where I spent many hours. Much of the information came from past editions of the Kidderminster Shuttle and from the world-wide-web.

My sincere thanks to Norman Tatlow, assisted by Tim Morris, who took on the task of proof reading and checking my script. My son Andrew, another former boy chorister, for his dedication and support in the preparation of the book layout and other technical things! Nigel Gilbert and the Hencroft Press for publication and my Carpet Museum Trust colleague, Richard Pugh-Cook, the Rev. Hugh Burton, Mrs Joyce Mathews and my wife, Shirley, who read the drafts.

Finally, yourself for buying the book and, in doing so, making a much-needed donation to the church funds.

Important dates and events

		Page
1818	Church Building Act 1818 passed through Parliament	13
1819	8th September - St.Mary's church vestry meeting agrees to build a church	15
1820	Architect Francis Goodwin appointed	18
1821	June - Architect William Knight appointed Clerk of Works	18
1821	19th July - foundations started	23
1821	28th August - foundation stone laid	23
1824	**13th September - St.George's Chapel and Burial Grounds were consecrated**	**23**
1824	***The Rev. W Villers - Curate in Charge***	***25***
1827	11th April - St.George's School foundation stone laid	30
1828	28th September - first organ dedicated in west gallery, organist appointed	27
1832	St.George's Chapel Choral Society formed	28
1842	***The Rev. J Downall - Curate in Charge***	***31***
1846	The Rev. William Walsham How - Assistant Curate	32
1847	***The Rev. T B Morrell - Curate in Charge***	***32***
1850	James Fitzgerald appointed organist and choirmaster	33
1852	30th July - Worcester Cross Infants School opens	34
1852	***The Rev. C J M Mottram - Curate in Charge***	***36***
1867	Parish of St.George formed	35
1867	***The Rev. C J M Mottram - Vicar***	***36***
1872	***The Rev. F R Evans - Vicar***	***45***
1873	January - first Parish Magazine	46
1873	Church closes for 4 weeks for major internal reconstruction	44
1873	New Hill organ west gallery	45
1876	Further internal improvements	49
1876	***The Rev. S B Bathe - Vicar***	***50***
1887	8th June - Parish Room foundation stone laid	54
1887	***The Rev. T W Church - Vicar***	***55***
1888	Ownership of Hoo Road Vicarage transferred to St.George's	56
1890	24th January - St.Andrew's Church opened under licence	58
1898	Organ relocated to northeast corner ground floor	51
1899	19th July - Leswell Street School foundation stone laid	59
1910	June - churchyard closed for burials	60
1912	10th April - Hoobrook Infants School foundation stone laid	61
1915	***The Rev. A E R Bedford - Vicar***	***64***
1916	18th April - dedication of a new choir vestry in the southeast corner of church	64
1916	Henry Radford becomes organist	65
1918	***The Rev. R H Stephen - Vicar***	***66***
1922	**20th November - St.George's Church destroyed by fire**	**67**
1923	Sir Giles Gilbert Scott appointed architect for restoration	76
1924	February - Grand Centenary Bazaar in Town Hall	74
1925	**13th September - St.George's Church rededicated**	**81**
1926	Harold Evers becomes organist and choirmaster	87
1928	St.George's Park opens	89
1928	28th May - first Whit Monday United Procession of Witness through town	89
1929	New Foskett organ installed above choir vestry	87
1929	15th Sept. - new east wall stained glass window dedicated to Good Mothers	88
1932	***The Rev. B J Isaac - Vicar***	***90***

1932	30th October - St.George's Men's Club formed, later Social Club	122
1933	Leswell Street Vicarage bought, Hoo Road Vicarage sold	91
1936	Acoustic improvements to church interior	92
1939	The Rev. Isaac becomes Army Chaplain	97
1940	***The Rev. P J Martin - Curate in Charge***	***97***
1945	***The Rev. P J Martin - Vicar***	***97***
1953	January - St.George's building is listed by Town & Country Planning	100
1956	23rd May - St.Chad's Church Hall dedicated	111
1957	17th March - All Saints' Chapel is dedicated	101
1957	13th October - first BBC Sunday Half Hour broadcast service from church	104
1959	***The Rev. L W Chidzey - Vicar***	***104***
1962	Hoobrook Church Hall opens	105
1962	Stewardship introduced	114
1960s	Worcester Cross School demolished	110
1963	5th May - new bells and mechanism dedicated	115
1967	26th November - St.Andrew's Church closes	107
1968	12th October - major organ restoration dedicated	118
1969	***The Rev. H E Montague-Youens - Vicar***	***119***
1969	Church of England moves to government by Synod	119
1971	St.Chad's extension	132
1973	St.George's building given Grade II* listing by English Heritage	100
1973	***The Rev. P D Chippendale - Vicar***	***124***
1974	June - St.George's Social Club moves to Radford Avenue	122
1975	Fifty Years Celebration since rededication	124
1976	Tim Morris appointed Organist and Choirmaster, Harold Evers retired	127
1977	***The Rev. J R Ilson - Rector***	***127***
1978	St.George's School closes and is demolished	110
1979	City of Birmingham Symphony Orchestra concerts in church	129
1981	17th July - the Church Annexe is dedicated	128
1983	Leswell Street School closes	111
1983	Formation of DCC and PCC	130
1983	30th January - TV Songs of Praise from St.Mary's broadcast	130
1985	More organ repairs	129
1985	Alternative Service Book [ASB] replaces Book of Common Prayer	131
1985	21st September - St.Chad's Church - more extensions dedicated	132
1986	***The Rev. N J W Barker - Rector***	***133***
1987	Major roof restoration work	133
1988	5th June - Rose "Peace Window" dedicated	134
1990	Restoration Fund started	136
1992	Fellowship Area created at west end church	140
1993	Clergy visit to Tanzania	136
1993	BBC Hereford & Worcester first Christmas Day broadcast	138
1994	Girls join choir	138
1994	6th October - St.Cecilia's Church extension dedicated	138
1995	Restoration work church tower	140
1996	***The Rev. H A Burton - Team Vicar***	***141***
2000	Part of roof replaced	142
2000	Interior completely redecorated, dorsal curtain removed	142
2001	16th September - dedication following major organ overhaul	143
2008	***The Rev. H A Burton - Team Rector Designate***	***147***

St. George's Church — Deanery of Kidderminster
Archdeaconry of Dudley — Diocese of Worcester

Sketch by Ken Jackson

We love the place, O God, wherein Thine honour dwells;
The joy of Thine abode, all earthly joy excels.
It is the house of prayer, wherein Thy servants meet;
And Thou, O Lord, art there, thy chosen flock to greet.
from Hymns Ancient & Modern 242.

Prologue

In the beginning

In the early years of the nineteenth century the population of the country was rapidly increasing and there was a concern by those in authority, that action was needed to satisfy the spiritual needs of ordinary folk.

Kidderminster in the 1820s

In 1820 Kidderminster had a population around 10,000. The manufacture of carpets was now the town's staple industry with twenty-two registered companies having their headquarters in Vicar Street, Church Street, Mill Street and around the Park Butts area - all on the River Stour. The canal, completed in 1772, provided the all-important transport link to and from the town.

Although Kidderminster was a thriving and growing town it should be remembered that the Industrial Revolution had not yet arrived. Families lived in court-style housing, mainly in the area around St.Mary's Church, Blackwell Street and the Horsefair.

Swan Street

However, the local authorities had not improved the amenities sufficiently to cater for the increasing population and the town had problems.

Dr. Thomas Thursfield, Surgeon to the Infirmary located in St.Mary's Street, described the town -
" ... *the courts and back streets are wretchedly bad. Cesspools are frequent and most of the drains are open on the surface, and with a very insufficient fall. The houses of the more improvident and poorer weavers are dirty, small, ill ventilated and wretched* ".

Handloom weaving shops were scattered around the town and child labour, both boys and girls, was a part of life. Thursfield continues -

"The workshops are generally well built, and, if kept clean, may be considered not unhealthy; but, owing to the dirt, the use of size in the carpets, and above all the want of common care in sweeping, on the part of the workmen - and lime washing, on the part of the masters, they are noisome holes. In the yard is usually one or more privies; these have, in most instances, open cesspools at the back, exhaling all sorts of effluvia."

In the carpet industry it was a time of conflict as the manufacturers, the Masters, were becoming rich with growing profits that were not shared with the workforce. The horse and cart provided the main means of transport around the town.
And so, with smoke from the chimneys, unkempt streets and a good number of alehouses coupled with a continual passage of townsfolk, Kidderminster could be described as a typical "Dickensian" style town.

High Street

Church of England attendance was for those who could afford the pew rents. The Town Church, St.Mary's, was the main stronghold. However, the Meeting House, founded by Richard Baxter, and other non-conformist chapels took the majority of the Sunday congregation in those days.

Kidderminster was typical of the growing towns in the country and against this backdrop Parliament decided to take action.

Church Building Act 1818

On the 6th February 1818 at the Freemasons' Hall in London a meeting, chaired by the Archbishop of Canterbury, considered a number of issues. One of the delegates, the Duke of Northumberland, proposed the formation of a Church Building Society, whose aim would be to lobby parliament for the provision of funds to build additional church buildings in the growing towns and cities throughout the country. Lord Kenyon seconded the proposal and the society was formed.
In the same year they successfully persuaded the Government to take action and the "Church Building Act 1818" subsequently passed through Parliament.

The Government saw the act as an opportunity to celebrate the successful conclusion of the Napoleonic Wars following the defeat of Napoleon by the Duke of

Wellington in June 1815. They set up a committee known as "Church Commissioners" [not the Church Commissioners of today] to undertake the selection of potential areas of growth and need.

An alternative view suggested that the "establishment" really wanted to curb a growth in non-conformity that was, at the time, associated with radical political views and they looked for areas of industrial growth and believed that the Church of England would stem this tide of dissent. It could be argued that this overview applied to Kidderminster.

Under the Church Building Act 1818, a sum of £1,000,000 was set aside. In the following years a further £500,000 was added and private finance added yet another £4,500,000.

Strict guidelines were set and the churches, known as "Waterloo" or "Commissioners" churches, were to be built to a rigid specification that required minimum cost and maximum seating. In those days church seating was reserved by the paying of a pew rent but the 1818 act stipulated that at least half the seats were to be provided free of charge for the poor.

The churches were often similar in style and many were dedicated to St.George, either as a tribute to the country's Patron Saint or George IV, whose Coronation was in 1821. Over 600 were built following the act and Kidderminster, with its rapidly developing carpet industry, was one of those towns selected.

View of Kidderminster from Aggborough c1780

The dictionary describes a church as a building for Christian worship or a body of Christians. A chapel is described as a private church. In the early chapters of this book both church, as a building, and chapel have the same meaning when applied to St.George's.

St. Mary's church vestry meeting 8th September 1819

Formal letters outlining the proposal were sent to the town but it was the responsibility of the local Church to put the wheels in motion. And so, the Venerable R.F Onslow MA, Archdeacon of Worcester and Vicar of Kidderminster called a meeting in St.Mary's and All Saints' church vestry and invited all the town's dignitaries.

He assumed the position of chairman and outlined the purpose of the meeting - "*For the purpose of taking into consideration the propriety of building a new Church or Chapel of Ease in the Parish of Kidderminster for the Accommodation of such Inhabitants as are precluded, by Want of Room, for attending Divine Worship in the Parish Church, and coming to such Resolutions on the subject as may be deemed expedient* ".

He commented on the growing population stating that, since the census of 1811 the population of the Borough had increased to 9283 and was still growing. He reported that the Parish Church could seat a maximum of 1400 in the pews using an allowance of 18 inches per person. With benches in the aisles a further 200 to 300 children could be accommodated. He remarked that there were no other consecrated chapels in the Borough, with the exception of Lower Mitton, that was capable of seating more than 450 persons.

An enthusiastic meeting discussed the issue and the following resolutions were agreed and recorded -

* "*The inhabitants of Kidderminster are precluded from attending Divine Worship by Want of Church-room* " and that a "*new Church should be erected on a spot of land belonging to BRECKNELL'S charity in Crabtree Closes* ".
* It should seat not less than 1500 persons with 1000 "*free sittings* ".
* A report of the meeting should be printed and sent to the Bishop of Worcester and the Rt. Hon. Thomas Lord Foley for their consent and approbation.
* Books should be prepared and left at the two banks for public subscriptions and Messrs. Wakeman, Farley and Turner are appointed treasurers.

These proposals were well received and today, in the County Record Office, there are many original letters of support from all sections of the community.

With the approval of the Bishop and Lord Foley the plan was set in motion for a "Chapel of Ease" to be built in the fields on the edge of town but within easy walking distance for the bulk of the population.

Working together - the project committee

A local committee was set up to work with the Church Commissioners. It was their responsibility to agree and appoint the architect, arrange for the builders and generally administer the outgoing costs. It was also their responsibility to arrange additional local funding and it soon became apparent that good support was forthcoming from many individuals including the "Masters" of the carpet industry.

The total building cost was estimated at £18,000 of which £2,000 was to be raised locally. The open fields, known as Crabtree Closes, were purchased for £800 from the trustees of Brecknell's Charity with money obtained from public subscription.

Note: In 1877 the road into Crabtree Closes was named Radford Avenue after Thomas Tempest Radford who, at the time, was a member of the congregation, a carpet Master and Mayor of Kidderminster in the years 1875, 1876 and 1886.

The sketch map below, surveyed and drawn by James Sherriff in 1780, shows a number of plots of land that were probably owned by the Foley family at the time.
Plot 129 eventually became the site for the new chapel.
The size was listed as being 3 acres, 3 rods and 5 poles.
In a separate document the land is recorded as being 190 feet above sea level.
The word "TUR....." refers to the Turnpike Road leading from town towards the Land Oak Toll house.

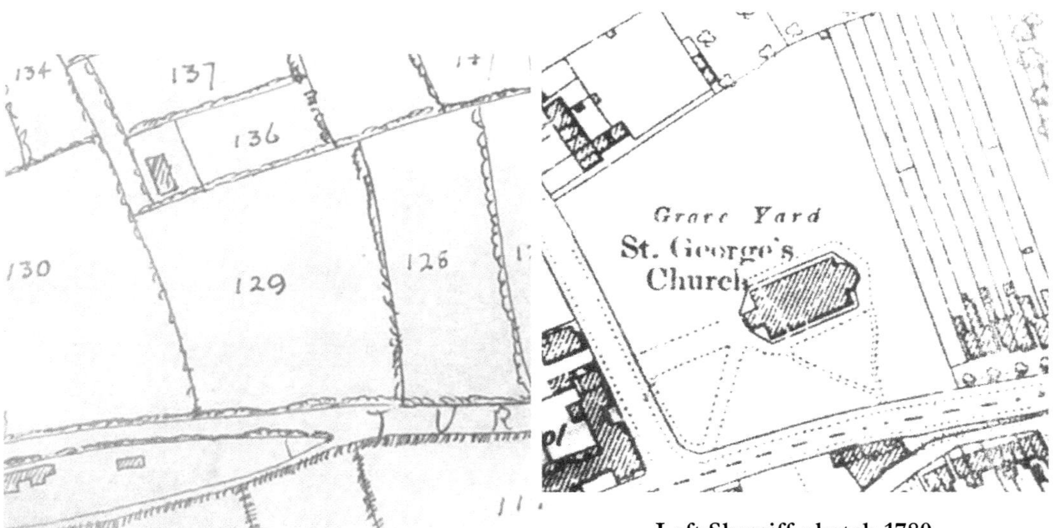

Left Sherriff sketch 1780
Above a plan dated 1902

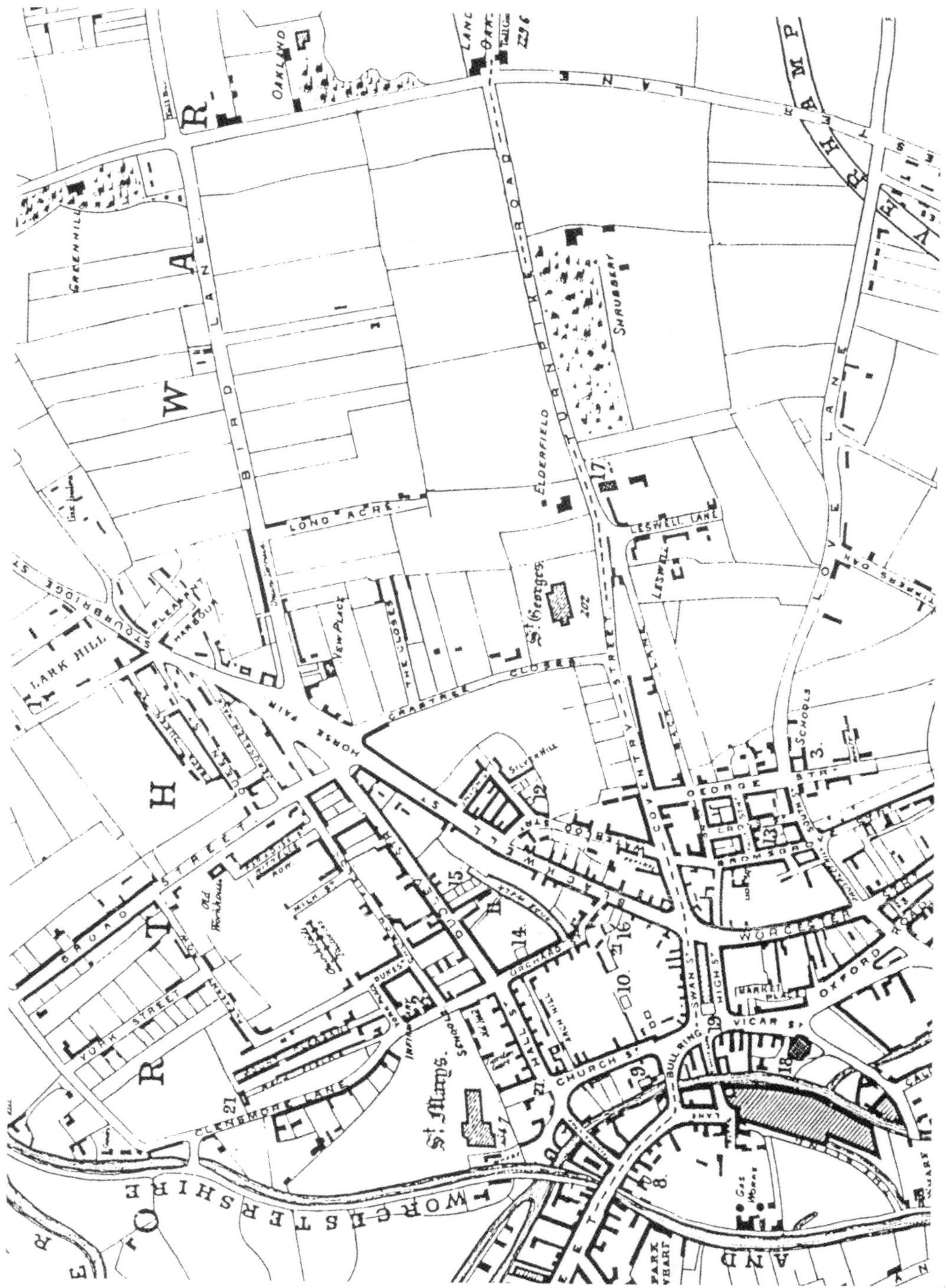

This map of the town, drawn by Borough Surveyor John Broadfield in 1859, shows the area selected for the building of St.George's Chapel and its relationship to St.Mary's and the populated area.
Note: Turnpike Road, Elderfield, the Shrubbery and Leswell Lane.

The architects

A number of architects were able to compete for the design of the Waterloo Churches. It appears that three were chosen to make proposals for St.George's namely Thomas Rickman, Francis Goodwin and Thomas Lee Junior. For a while the latter was the favourite with his "*oak pewing and Norman architecture* " whereas Goodwin and Rickman preferred a Gothic influence. The committee eventually chose Goodwin's design for its "*elegance, strength and durability* ". Francis Goodwin was known for his aggressive business tactics and these could have played a part in the final decision!

Francis Goodwin

Francis Goodwin [1784-1835] was born in Kings Lynn. He designed the first Manchester Town Hall but is best known for the Waterloo Churches he built in many parts of the country. He used what was called a "Gothic revival" style. His local contact and clerk of works was another architect named William Knight who came with a good reputation.

William Knight

Architect William Knight [1780-1845] was not a native of Kidderminster, but he had gained a reputation in the area for his competence in the supervision of the construction of large buildings to the designs of others. He was appointed Clerk of Works in June 1821 at a salary of £100 per annum.

Both architects were present at the laying of the foundation stone and, after the consecration, Knight was granted a £20 bonus in recognition for his outstanding work. William Knight went on to supervise other projects in Worcestershire, including an expansion to St.Michael's Church in Stourport and St.James' at Hartlebury. But he chose St.George's, which he described as one of his greatest achievements, for his final resting place. He died in September 1845 and his sandstone tomb can be found on the left-hand side of the current tree-lined drive. Today, the inscriptions are totally illegible but originally read - "*Sacred, To the Memory of William Knight, Architect. Who died 7th September 1845 aged 65 years. This Church, erected Under his superintendence, Stands A lasting Monument Of his Integrity and Skill* ".
There is also an inscription to the memory of his wife, Catherine, who was also buried in the tomb.
The location is marked **WK** on the graveyard plan in Chapter 3 page 39.

Entrance porch, tower, bells and clock

By design St.George's was perpendicular in style with stone faces and cast iron window frames. The exterior was also described as being "Georgian Gothic" with elaborate gabled buttresses and towers with turrets and pinnacles.

The main entrance was via two large doors into a spacious porch area. The porch was directly under the magnificent tall tower that is still visible today from most parts of the town. A second set of doors gave access to the body of the church.

With the restrictions on expenditure coupled with its close proximity to St.Mary's and its fine peal of bells, St.George's bells were basic and practical.
At high level, three bells, cast at John Rudhall's Gloucester foundry, hung in the tower. The largest was 47 inches diameter and weighed 17 cwt. [0.85 Ton].
It was inscribed - "*St.George's Chapel produced at the expense of the Parish of Kidderminster 1825. Rev. R.F Onslow DD Archdeacon of Worcester, Vicar of Kidderminster; Rev. Wm. Villers BA perpetual curate of St.George's Chapel; Samuel Beddows, Thomas Peverall, John C Crane, James Dovey Churchwardens; J Rudhall. Fecit* ".
The second, 30 inches diameter, weighed 5 cwt. and the third, 17 inches diameter, weighed just over 1 cwt. Both were inscribed with the manufacturers name and date.

The supply order listed two biers, planks, ropes and ladders. The long ropes reached to the ground and the bells could be rung from the porch area or from the bell chamber above.

In those days the church clock played an important role in the time keeping of local people. St.George's had three clock faces positioned in the lower part of the tower on the north, south and west faces.

In the photograph, taken from the north side around 1900, the clock is clearly visible showing the time at 3.55 pm.

Note: the established trees and the well-populated graveyard.

The clock mechanisms protruded on the internal walls of the tower and would have been wound, maintained and set from the first floor level. The presence of the clocks has often been the subject of debate since there are no records of their purchase and installation nor do they feature in the majority of photographs. While the photograph on page 19 proves the point, there was also support from the *Brierley Hill Advertiser* who reported on a fire at Clensmore Flour Mill in the early hours of 23rd June 1858 - "... *so great was the glare from the fire that the clocks of St.Mary's and St.George's were clearly visible* ".

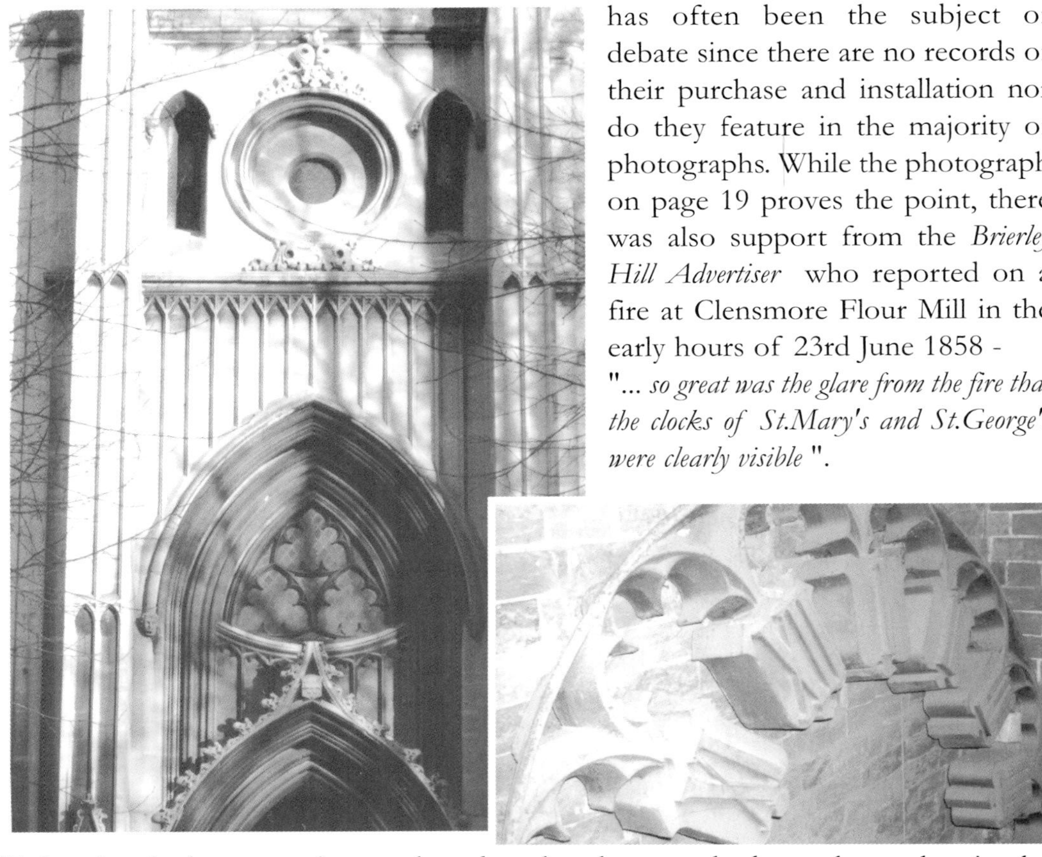

Today the clocks are no longer there but the photograph above shows the circular recesses that are still in place, now secure with leaded glass. It is probable that the clocks were completely destroyed in the 1922 fire and were not replaced. Today, on the floor of the bell chamber lie three Roman numeral clock faces!

Foundations, stonework and the body of the church

In keeping with the design of large buildings stone played an important part. The foundations were described as being of Gornal Stone. The walls were of brick construction plastered internally and faced externally with Bath Stone. The porch floor was Painswick Stone relieved with Bidford Stone. The nave aisles again used Painswick Stone. The raised chancel area was accessed via stone steps and part was decorated with red and black tiles. These tiles can be seen in the photograph on page 43. Some of the white stone blocks were surplus to requirements and these are said to have been used for the foundation of the high Coventry Street wall supporting Elderfield Gardens - they are still visible from the road!

A traditional pitched timber and tile roof spanned the main body of the church. Inside a full-width tent-like feature ceiling provided a degree of insulation and helped with the acoustics.
In Chapter 3, internal views looking towards the east altar wall show the rose window and the line of the ceiling above it. What cannot be seen is the triangular window above the rose window, which gave some light and ventilation to the cavity between the ceiling and the underside of the roof. This triangular window is visible from the outside in the photograph above. In fact there were three windows of this design. The first can be seen in the previous photograph being part of the main feature over the existing porch entry. A second window was positioned opposite the first to provide some light between the porch and the west gallery. This second window has its own story to tell in a later chapter.

St.George's in Kidderminster, with a total of 2000 seats, was one of the largest Waterloo Churches built in the country. 1200 of the pew seats were free. In the nave of the church, carved wooden "horsebox" pews packed every possible space. On the north, south and west walls was a spacious wooden gallery supported on cast iron columns. The gallery contained pew seating for 650 people and was accessed by staircases in the northwest and southwest corners. These staircases could also be reached from the churchyard via the two heavy timber doors. The door location still exists today.

Good natural lighting was provided at both levels from the tall windows positioned on the north and south walls. Initially, it is probable that candles and oil lamps provided the artificial lighting although the lamps would have had little effect with such a large space. Heating came from a large coal-fired stove positioned near the west entrance doors.

The chancel was much smaller than it is today and, in the sanctuary, a door to the right of the altar gave access to a clergy vestry that was built onto the rear. This door was the clergy's only internal entrance to the church for the services. The vestry was self-contained with its own fireplace. It also had a door entrance from the churchyard that can clearly be seen in the photograph.

The altar was the central feature on the east wall. An altarpiece depicting "*The Descent from the Cross* " was woven at Bowyer's town centre carpet factory. It is recorded that the carpet was designed by Joseph Bowyer himself and contained a "*considerable brilliance of colour and elegance of design* ". Within two years of the consecration of the church it had been vandalised and was replaced by "*The Lord's Prayer, the Creed, and the Ten Commandments* ". Unfortunately, there is no pictorial record of either.
Directly above the altar was the large circular rose window with two smaller plain glass windows nearer the corners giving light to the upper galleries.

Early records describe a font at the rear of the church that stood on a York Stone base and platform. It was constructed with an octagonal stone bowl supported on a thick green Connemara marble column with eight smaller Numidian red marble columns clustered around it. Another church treasure was a silver collection plate, 12 inches diameter by 4 inches deep, hallmarked 1824. Engraved with a relief design of re-occurring flowers and leaves, with bead formation on the extreme edge, it was inscribed - "*Sacrum Altari Aedis Santre [or Sanctae] Rei Publicae Munificentia Et Civium Kiddermins Liberalitate In Oppido Suo Nuperrime Positae MDCCCXXIV* " with "*IHS* " motif set in centre of the inscription. A translation from the Latin reads -
"*Sacred to the Altar of the Holy Temple recently built in the town, through the munificence of the civic authorities and the generosity of the citizens of Kidderminster 1824* ".

The land contained ample area for graves with the churchyard totally surrounding the church. Tall trees were planted around the perimeter and bordering the driveway.
A low wall enclosed the whole area with a capping stone into which were embedded wrought iron railings. The main church driveway, with a good pair of gates, started in Coventry Street near the junction with Crabtree Closes. Another pathway cut across the churchyard to join Coventry Street near the southeast corner.

Foundations and building work

Although the digging of the foundations started on the 19th July 1821, the day of the Coronation of King George IV, it was not until the 28th August that a proper foundation stone was laid by the Venerable R.F Onslow, Vicar of Kidderminster.

The church took thirty-eight months to complete and it must have been an exciting time for those who were able to watch the growth of the structure as the bricklayers, stonemasons, carpenters and labourers toiled away. It is probable that the canal was the main route to the town for the majority of the materials, with horse-drawn wagons making the final leg up the hill from the town wharfs.
It must also have been spectacular to see the stone sections of the tower being manually hoisted into position via the timber scaffolding and the rope and pulley systems. When the building was near completion the finishing touches would have come from those involved with the decoration of the inside; the bricklayers building the perimeter walls and the gardeners preparing the burial ground, laying out the paths and planting the trees.

Unfortunately, there are no written records, drawings or sketches of this active period except for two stories that required action by the committee. The first concerned the bankruptcy of one of the contractors who had to be replaced. The second was about a workman who fell from the tower into a pit of cement. Fortunately, it had a happy ending because he was unhurt and the committee awarded him a medal for his services.

Consecration Service - 13th September 1824

St.George's Chapel and Burial Grounds were consecrated 13th September 1824

The Rt. Rev. Folliott Herbert Walker Cornewall DD, Lord Bishop of Worcester led the service assisted by the Rev. William Villers who was appointed the first Curate in Charge of St.George's Chapel.

Again, there are no records of the service itself except for some extracts from the choral part of the service. However, in the clergy vestry there is a commemoration medal and a framed gallery ticket for the service. Costing one shilling it requests - "*Person attending must be in their seat by eleven o'Clock* ". The medal wording can be found in the Appendix.

Imagine the scene before the service as 2000 souls made their way to St.George's. The tolling of the bells and the hubbub of people dressed in their Sunday best coming on foot and being escorted to their seats.

The gentry and their ladies arriving by horse and carriage - perhaps they had to line up in Crabtree Closes waiting their turn to make the grand entrance to their allotted pew seats.

The wardens and church officers known as the "beadles" would have been extremely busy making sure that things were going according to plan. The Rev. W Villers, the Bishop and other clergy would have been in the vestry making final adjustments as they prepared for the service.

By today's standards, and in the knowledge that so many people would be attending, it seems incredible that no permanent provision was made for any music. However, the church committee did authorise Rev. W Villers and Mr. J Hallen to make arrangements for hiring "*vocal and instrumental performers* " to lead the consecration service at a total cost not to exceed £50. A Mr. Charles Mathews was also involved in the selection.

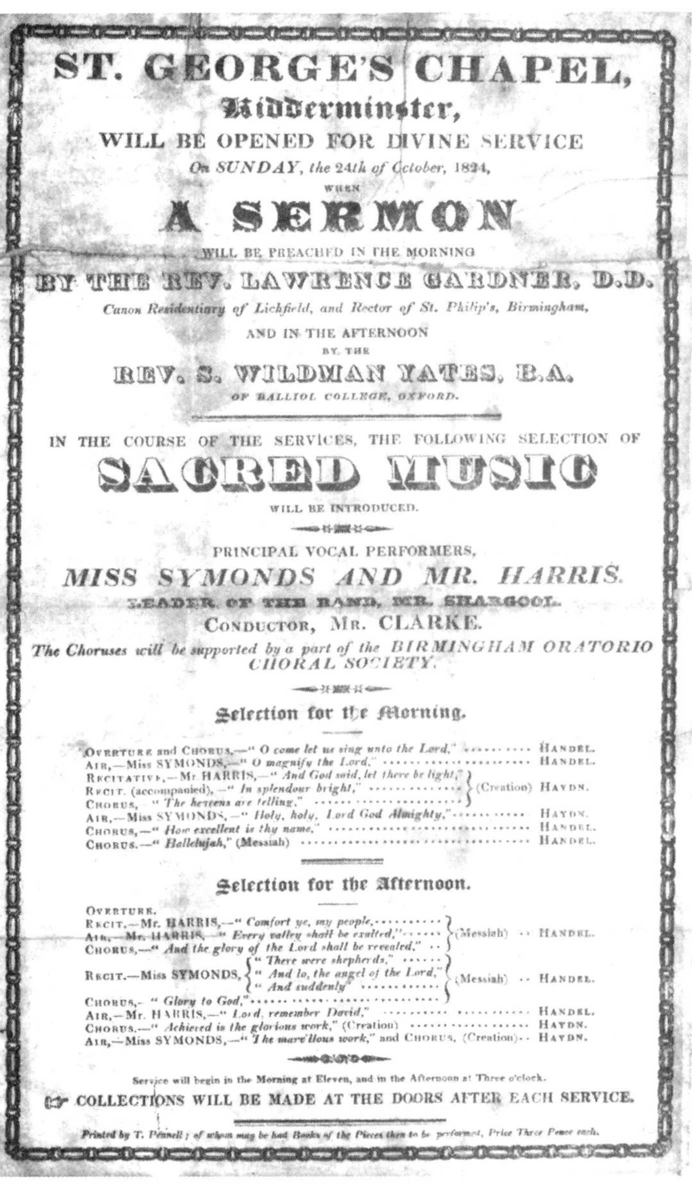

ST. GEORGE'S CHAPEL,
Kidderminster,
WILL BE OPENED FOR DIVINE SERVICE
On SUNDAY, the 24th of October, 1824,
WHEN
A SERMON
WILL BE PREACHED IN THE MORNING
BY THE REV. LAWRENCE GARDNER, D.D.
Canon Residentiary of Lichfield, and Rector of St. Philip's, Birmingham,
AND IN THE AFTERNOON
BY THE
REV. S. WILDMAN YATES, B.A.
OF BALLIOL COLLEGE, OXFORD.

IN THE COURSE OF THE SERVICES, THE FOLLOWING SELECTION OF
SACRED MUSIC
WILL BE INTRODUCED.

PRINCIPAL VOCAL PERFORMERS,
MISS SYMONDS AND MR. HARRIS.
LEADER OF THE BAND, MR. SHARGOOL.
CONDUCTOR, MR. CLARKE.
The Choruses will be supported by a part of the BIRMINGHAM ORATORIO CHORAL SOCIETY.

Selection for the Morning.

OVERTURE and CHORUS,—" *O come let us sing unto the Lord,*" .... HANDEL.
AIR,—Miss SYMONDS,—" *O magnify the Lord,*" .... HANDEL.
RECITATIVE,—Mr. HARRIS,—" *And God said, let there be light,*"
RECIT. (accompanied),—" *In splendour bright,*" .... (Creation) HAYDN.
CHORUS, " *The heavens are telling,*" ....
AIR,—Miss SYMONDS,—" *Holy, holy, Lord God Almighty,*" .... HAYDN.
CHORUS,—" *How excellent is thy name,*" .... HANDEL.
CHORUS.—" *Hallelujah,*" (Messiah) .... HANDEL.

Selection for the Afternoon.

OVERTURE.
RECIT.—Mr. HARRIS,—" *Comfort ye, my people,*" ....
AIR,—Mr. HARRIS,—" *Every valley shall be exalted,*" .... (Messiah) .. HANDEL.
CHORUS,—" *And the glory of the Lord shall be revealed,*" ..
RECIT.—Miss SYMONDS, " *There were shepherds,*" .... " *And lo, the angel of the Lord,*" " *And suddenly*" .... (Messiah) .. HANDEL.
CHORUS,— " *Glory to God,*" ....
AIR,—Mr. HARRIS,—" *Lord, remember David,*" .... HANDEL.
CHORUS.—" *Achieved is the glorious work,*" (Creation) .... HAYDN.
AIR,—Miss SYMONDS,—" *The marv'llous work,*" and CHORUS, (Creation).. HAYDN.

Service will begin in the Morning at Eleven, and in the Afternoon at Three o'clock.
COLLECTIONS WILL BE MADE AT THE DOORS AFTER EACH SERVICE.

Printed by T. Pennell; of whom may be had Books of the Pieces then to be performed, Price Three Pence each.

Following the church's consecration a normal pattern of services was put in place. On Sunday 24th October 1824 there was another special celebration service with "*Sermon and Sacred Music*". It was well advertised as can be seen in the poster.

Note: These two October services were held in the morning at 11.00 am and in the afternoon at 3.00 pm.

The Rev. William Villers BA
The first Curate in Charge 1824-1842

William Villers was an active man and played a leading part in the establishment of St.George's Chapel. The biggest mystery surrounding him seems to be the spelling of his surname. The stone plaque in church records "Villiers" as does the council road sign at the entrance of "Villiers Street", named after him. But the old blue enamel plaque on the house wall near the Chester Road junction reverts to "Villers".

The Rev. William Villers, Perpetual Curate of St. George's, Kidderminster, 1824–1842.

VILLIER'S STREET

Perhaps the casting vote should be in his signature that frequently appears in the minute books and the church registers.

Resolved, That the Minister be requested to select such Psalms & Hymns as he may think proper to be introduced into the Services of the following Sundays —

Wm Villers.
Chairman.

Little is known about his private life. However, a Mrs Villers, presumably his wife, is credited for passing on second-hand clothing to the poor children working in the town's carpet industry. This is the only reference found to any other member of the family. William himself was popular, and so his congregation presented him with a magnificent silver plate on Monday 26th September 1836 at a gathering chaired by the new Mayor of Kidderminster, William Butler Best.

After 18 years in charge he left in 1842. It is probable that he moved to Bromsgrove where it is recorded in 1846 that a Rev. W Villers was Vicar of Bromsgrove and later, in 1853, appointed Honorary Canon of Worcester Cathedral.

Layout of the pews

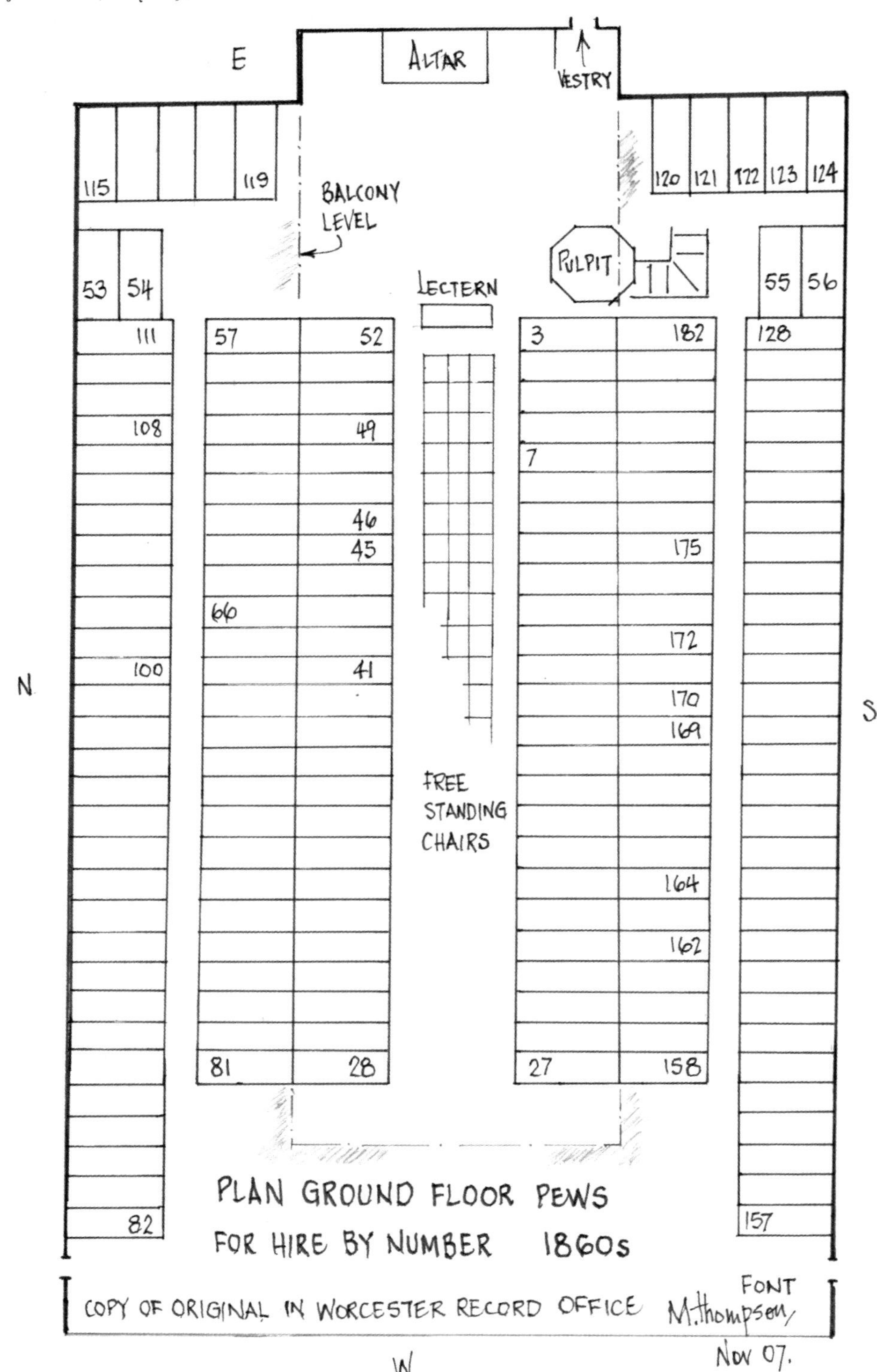

The St.George's document deposit in the County Records Office contains two interesting and informative undated ground-floor seating layouts - a sketch of the first is shown opposite. Recorded during the time of the Rev. C.J.M Mottram [1852-1872] it confirms the desire to use all available space. All the ground floor rows are numbered and to the side are the names of those who have rented the pews. The upper gallery is not shown and it is probable that this was part of the free seating allocation.
Extracts from the list -

7 Charles Dixon
41 Mr Crane "Habberley"
45 Edward Hughes [carpets]
46 Rev. C.J.M Mottram
49 Charles Harvey
52 W Grazebrook "Park Hall"
66 Mansel "The Lamb"
100 Schoolteachers
108 C Harvey's servants
119 Mr Viney [churchwarden]
121 & 122 F Jefferies [carpets]
157 Beadles
162 Hughes "The Closes"
164 Kent Schoolmaster
169 Grazebrook's servants
170 Wilson "Hodge Hill"
172 Rev. Mottram's servants
175 Hasell [Silver Street]

The beadles sat at the back and the story is told that St.George's also employed a "*nobbler*" who was dressed in a blue uniform and walked around the church during services to control the unruly and wake up those who had fallen asleep.

One of the congregation was Charles Harvey who, together with his brother John, were local wine merchants with premises at No.1 Coventry Street. Their business was also centred in Bristol and it was from there that the famous Harvey's Bristol Cream Sherry was introduced. For a period he was the owner of Elderfield House which is the large white house at the top of the hill on the left overlooking the churchyard [see Broadfield 1859 map]. The names Pardoe and Hooman also appear in the early house deeds.

The first Organ and Choir

The committee soon realised that an organ and choir was essential to lead the worship. Within the first few months a small choir had been formed and they sat together in seats reserved for them. The introduction of an organ was not so easy. It took time to consider the specification, obtain quotations and raise the necessary finance and it was not until some years later that the first organ was installed.

The exact specification is unclear but an old invoice from Elliot & Hill reads - "*1828 April - St.George's new church organ, Kidderminster. Ordered by the Rev. W Villers £550-0-0d* ". Subsequently, the organ was installed by William Hill and Company of London who were eminent organ builders of the day. It was positioned at the centre of the west gallery above the entrance doors. This was the usual location for organs in those days.
Note: The Town Hall also has a Hill Organ that was installed after St.George's in 1855.

At the organ dedication service on 28th September 1828 the Rev. W.F Hook DD preached a powerful sermon. At the time, the Rev. Hook was Vicar of Holy Trinity in Coventry but went on to become Vicar of Leeds and President of the Leeds Philosophical and Literary Society.

Church committees

From the records of the early church committee meetings it is apparent that some influential town businessmen were attracted to join the new congregation. Names like John and Charles Harvey together with the carpet manufacturers of the day Woodward, Morton, Humphries, Whittall, Hooman and Holmes.

The committees considered all matters, for example, in 1833 they became concerned that the largest of the tower bells was cracked and so they obtained an estimate from John Rudhall that read - "*To Messrs J Harvey & H Woodward, Church Wardens, St.George's Chapel, Kidderminster. Take down and recast the broken bell, fit the present wheel, clapper and stock and hang the bell for £35* ". The quotation was accepted and a new bell was hung in June 1834.

It was a time of expansion for the town's carpet industry and new housing was needed. Land Clubs were formed to purchase land and build affordable housing. St.George's Land Club was one of these and it is probable that the church had some influence.
The Rev. William Villers was involved in the early years for the purchase of land titled "St.George's Fields" which was near the proposed new railway line. In the late 1850s some housing had been built in what today is known as Lorne Street and Villiers Street.

One of the stalwarts of the early committees was George Hooman who was a successful businessman being a partner with the carpet manufacturers and yarn spinners Pardoe, Hooman & Pardoe. At the time his company was the largest in town. He was also Mayor of Kidderminster in 1837 and again in 1845. He served St.George's well and sat on a number of committees including the St.George's Chapel Choral Society.

St. George's Chapel Choral Society

In the church archive, a leather-bound ledger entitled "*St.George's Chapel Choral Society Rules*" and "*Accounts*" records, in copperplate handwriting, the minutes charting the formation of the choral society under the leadership of the Rev. William Villers.

The volume records the names of the original eighteen members of the choir in 1825 of whom six were ladies. The names are reproduced in the Appendix.
On a separate page, dated June 1832, the objects of the society are set out - "*St.George's Chapel Kidderminster is provided with a very excellent organ and it must surely be considered desirable for the decent performance of Divine Worship that an efficient organist and choir be also provided. It is considered that £50 per annum will be required to effect this desirable end; towards this sum the Rev. W Villers promises that two sermons shall be preached and collections made at the doors of the Chapel annually on the last Sunday in May, unless the Sacrament should be administered on that day, in which case, the sermons should be preached on the preceding Sunday. If the produce of these sermons should not amount to £50 annually we the undersigned do hereby pledge ourselves to make up the deficiency by equal subscription*".

There followed forty names of the town's business elite, all gentlemen.

The ledger goes on recording the plan of action -
"*It is resolved that - a committee be annually selected by the seat holders for the management of the choir and for the receipt and expenditure of any monies contributed for its support. It is further resolved that - in the event of the collections exceeding £50 the surplus be presented to the organist* ".
The first elected committee was Mr. Morton, Mr. Mathews, Mr. Hallen, Mr. Bradley, Mr. Latham and the aforementioned George Hooman.
It appears that, in the early years, the organist and the choirmaster were two different individuals and both were paid positions. The choristers also received a payment. With two people in office conflict was inevitable and so the committee laid a set of rules for both. The organist, as well as playing for services, should also attend and play at the choir practice. The choirmaster must set aside one evening each week, other than Sunday, for the instruction of the choristers. It was also his job to select the psalms and hymns for each service and submit them to the committee for approval.
The names of the early choirmasters are not clearly recorded with the exception of a Mr. Grant, who was in office in 1832 on a salary of £7. 10 shillings and, later, a Mr. Sam Renny.

The first Organists

With the organ installed in the west gallery the first organist, appointed in 1828, was a Mr Manwill who retained the position for four years. His departure caused a problem because a local replacement was not easy to find. Adverts in the Birmingham Gazette, Morning Herald and Worcester Journal attracted replies from as-far--field as County Galway in Ireland and Newcastle-on-Tyne. Eventually, in 1832, Mr. George Hay was appointed but he resigned within his first year and a William Ward took the position, but he only stayed for one month.
The committee needed professional help and they contacted Charles Clarke the organist at Worcester Cathedral and he was able to supply a Mr. Done on a temporary appointment. He proved to be suitable and was offered a permanent position but declined the offer. And so the committee took their time before appointing Mr. W.H Rogers who added some stability and remained for the next twenty-two years serving between 1833 and 1855. It is probable that during this period the positions of organist and choirmaster became one.
The Chapel Choral Society Committee continued to maintain a close control over the music and the organist. At a meeting in the late 1830s they considered a "*Scheme of Music*" put forward by the organist that did not meet with their full approval and it was resolved that, in future "*Mr. Rogers should meet the Committee at the Organ at seven o'clock on Friday Evenings for the purpose of making a selection of tunes to be adapted to the different Psalms and Hymns used in this Chapel* ". Another resolution requested, "*Mr. Rogers should in all cases strictly adhere to the Written Music contained in the Compositions which may at any time be introduced into the Service*". The final resolution clearly sums up the situation and real intention, "*That the Minister be requested to select such Psalms and Hymns as he may think proper to be introduced into the Services of the following Sundays* ". The minutes were written and signed by the Chairman, the Rev. Wm Villers. This latter section is reproduced in the Rev. Villers' profile on page 25.

St. George's School

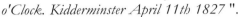

The need for good schooling was a national problem and St.George's immediately took up the challenge and formed yet another committee which posted the following notice - "*St.George's National Sunday and Day Schools -*
The COMMITTEE having made such arrangements as will enable them to commence building th above schools on Monday next, the 16th inst. request the attendance of SUBSCRIBERS an FRIENDS in general to the Education of the Poor in the Principles of the ESTABLISHED CHURCH, on the occasion of LAYING the FIRST STONE, which is to take place at Twelve o'Clock. Kidderminster April 11th 1827 ".

The first of St.George's Schools was built in George Street on the corner with th intersection with Love Lane [renamed Offmore Road in 1886]. A foundation plaque o the end wall read "*St.George's National Sunday and Day Schools erected 1827* ".

In the 22nd April 1827 edition of the John Bull newspaper the following was written [not the elaborate wording] "*Kidderminster - On Monday last was laid the first stone of the Nation Sunday and Day Schools belonging to St.George's Chapel in the Borough of Kidderminster. Th interesting ceremonial took place in the presence of a large concourse of persons assembled to witness i Immediately after Divine Service, the High Bailiff and Corporation, preceded by the children of th charity schools, and attended by the Clergy, Church Wardens, and a very numerous and respectab assembly of ladies and gentlemen of the town and neighbourhood, proceeded from St.George's Chapel t the site of the intended building, where, the plans of the edifice having been exhibited, the stone w lowered into the situation prepared for it and fixed there with all the forms customary upon such occasion. The Rev. Wm Villers, the Minister of St.George's Chapel, then offered short but suitable prayer for th blessing of Divine Providence upon the charitable design, and for the future success of the Institution, th children, having repeated the Lord's Prayer, in a devout and becoming manner.*
The Rev. T Cook the highly respected curate of the Parish, delivered a very eloquent and appropria address, at the conclusion of which one of committee returned thanks for the kind interest which ha displayed by the persons present in the commencement and future prosperity of the New Establishment ".

By local standards the school was large. An attendance list dated 1870 records that th school had places for 200 boys and 165 girls. The photographs were taken in 1968. Note: The smaller building to the right is the Parish Room - details in Chapter 5.

In 1932 architects Pritchard, Goodwin & Clist surveyed three old cottages bordering the playground. Known as "Smith's Cottages" they were purchased and subsequently demolished to enlarge the playground.

Additional Services

Church services continued to be well attended under the leadership of the Rev. W Villers. The records indicate that they were mainly held at times when natural light prevailed. This was probably because of the inefficiency of the candles and oil lamps in such a large building. It will be recalled that the October Consecration Services were held in the morning and afternoon only. This fact did not deter a group of individuals who, in 1835, got together to arrange additional services for Sunday Evenings.

From the church archives a bound book records the minutes of a series of meetings held to discuss the matter. The chairman was the Rev. W Villers and inside the front cover it reads - "*The names hereunto subscribed are willing to contribute the sums set opposite our respective names for the purpose of providing the necessary expenses of an additional Service at St.George's on Sunday Evenings* ".
A list of names, payments and dates follows. The book covers the years 1835 - 1838.

The Rev. John Downall MA - Curate in Charge 1842-1847

After eighteen years in office the Rev. William Villers left St.George's. In 1842 he was succeeded by another Curate in Charge, the Rev. John Downall, who remained for the next five years. Apart from the fact that he was educated at Magdalen Hall, Oxford very little is known about him or his ministry.
In 1847 he was appointed Vicar of Oakhampton and later Rural Dean of Totnes and Canon in the Cathedral Church of Exeter.

The Weavers' Strike

Four years after the consecration of the church the weavers of the carpet industry were in conflict with the masters over payment for the woven yard. Without any consultation the masters introduced a significant reduction and, in 1828, the nationally reported strike of the weavers of Kidderminster took place and lasted twenty-one weeks.

During the strike the weavers gained the support of the Kidderminster born the Rev. Humphrey Price who was Vicar of Needwood near Lichfield. However, the Kidderminster clergy appear to have kept a low profile.

Perhaps this is understandable since the masters were the church's main benefactors. But in the years following the Rev. W Villers did comment on the conduct of the weavers. He said - *"During the continuance of the strike habits of idleness, drunkenness, gamboling and a general recklessness of conduct were acquired"* much to the disgust of the weavers in his congregation.

The Rev. J Downall arrived in 1842 and, being new to the district, was approached by the weavers' committee who were still fighting to improve their lot. He agreed to meet the masters and appeal to them *"as christians"*. His discussions were also fruitless and they convinced him that any increase would lead to *"the entire suspension of employment"*. Having failed with this approach the weavers reported the matter at a mass meeting.

The Rev. Thomas Baker Morrell MA - Curate in Charge 1847-1852

The Rev. Thomas Baker Morrell took office in 1847. Educated at Balliol College, Oxford he was in his thirties when he came to St.George's. According to the 1851 census return, he lived with his housekeeper and two servants at a vicarage that belonged to St.Mary's in Hoo Lane. In 1851 he is also listed as being Principal at a "Diocesan Commercial School" located at Spring Bank House in Leswell Lane. The house overlooked Coventry Street and the southeast corner of the churchyard. He left the town in 1852 to become vicar of Henley-on-Thames.

Assistant Curates

Over a number of years the vicar of St.Mary's, the Rev. Thomas L Claughton, was known to provide guidance and advice to a number of curates in training. This arrangement was ideal for St.George's and some interesting individuals were attracted to the area, if only for a short time.

One of these was a young man who came to St.George's for his first curacy following his ordination in 1846. His name was William Walsham How and he went on to become a prolific hymn writer and ultimately the first Bishop of Wakefield.
During his lifetime he wrote over 50 hymns including "Soldiers of Christ, Arise!" [A&M 305] and "It is a thing most wonderful" [A&M 360]. His most famous hymn was "For All the Saints" [A&M 527] sung to Vaughan Williams's tune "Sine Nomine".

He remained in Kidderminster for two years and during that time compiled the "Daily Family Prayers for Churchmen" and collaborated with the Rev. Morrell to write a book of "Psalms and Hymns" - both were published in 1854.
Another senior curate to make his mark was the Rev. B Gibbons whose name was associated with all aspects of church life. He took an active interest in the development of the schools and his name appears many times in the church registers. For a time he was Chairman of the Chapel Choral Society and, in 1854, he presented the church with a handsome silver-gilt alms dish.
There were other assistant curates whose names were not formally listed in the church records. In the appendix of this book some have been recorded, as their names became known during the research.

The Rev. Charles John MacQueen Mottram MA - Curate in Charge 1852-1867

Following the Rev. Morrell's departure in 1852 the Rev. Charles John MacQueen Mottram took office. He was another student of Magdalen Hall, Oxford before he joined St.Mary's as a curate under the tutorage of the Rev. T L Claughton.
In 1852 he was appointed Curate in Charge of St.George's and came at an important period in the growth of the town. For the next fifteen years he retained the position and it was under his leadership that the church was to take a significant step forward.
For the majority of his ministry his organist and choirmaster was a young James Fitzgerald.

James Fitzgerald - Organist and Choirmaster for 45 years

James Fitzgerald was born in the same year as St.George's Chapel was consecrated. He developed an interest in music and became an organ scholar. While in his early twenties, he took an appointment as organist at St.Mary's Church.
Although St.George's Chapel was autonomous for its day-to-day working it still retained a close relationship with its parent and it was probably this relationship that led to an agreement that saw Fitzgerald sharing his organ skills. From 1850 and for the next seventeen years he was officially organist and choirmaster for both churches. It goes without saying that some assistance would have been necessary when the services coincided.
In 1867, when the Parish of St.George was formed, James Fitzgerald decided to devote the rest of his career to St.George's and he immediately took a more active roll in church affairs. In his private life he lived in Leswell Terrace.

Fitzgerald was a Freemason and he retained an interest in all forms of choral singing. In 1850 he formed the Kidderminster Choral Society.

He died in 1895 and is buried in the southeast part of the churchyard where it is carved on his memorial gravestone that he was organist for 45 years.
[location **JF** on graveyard plan in Chapter 3 page 39].

Worcester Cross School

The growing town needed more schools and in 1852 another was built on the edge of town at the bottom of Hoo Lane [Road] at Worcester Cross. Finance came from a generous donation by the Senior Curate of St.George's, the Rev. B Gibbons. The land was a donation from the Rev. T.L Claughton, Vicar of Kidderminster. At the time the Glebe [belonging to the church] meadowland behind the school and towards the Back Brook branch of the River Stour was being considered for the building of Stour Vale Mill which was specially designed for the new power-looms. The factory was completed in 1855 and in later years it was known as the home of Woodward Grosvenor. Today, it is the location of the town's Carpet Museum.

The first school building was described as "*a single school room with a house beneath* ". It opened as an Infants School on 30th July 1852. In 1871 it was enlarged with the addition of another classroom and a teacher's house. The new school was designed to accommodate 50 mixed juniors and 80 infants. A night school was provided during the winter months.

It was another impressive school-like building with elaborate brickwork forming the gable end. At the apex, a cross, and below the engraved inscription - "*THE FEAR OF THE LORD IS THE BEGINNING OF WISDOM* ".

In the early years the school building was an integral part of church life with regular services every Friday at 7.30 pm while the Men's Bible Class met on Tuesday evenings.

The 1968 photograph shows its location at the bottom of Hoo Road near the intersection with Green Street.

Chapter 3 The Parish of St. George formed in 1867

Growing Town

The introduction of the power looms in the early 1850s changed the face of the town as the mills and factories were built for the metal looms driven by steam engines. By 1867 the population had grown to nearer 20,000 and so it was decided to create the Parish of St.George.

It was large and took in most of the south side of the town centre. Coventry Street was the boundary with St.Mary's Parish and a detour around the churchyard was necessary to ensure that St.George's Church was in its own parish. The new parish boundary extended to the developing areas of Hoobrook and Offmore.

Today, it seems odd that a parish church should be so far from the centre of parish life. But, it must be remembered that, in 1824, St.George's Chapel was on the edge of town and ideally placed to serve the community of the day.

The new District Chapelry of Saint George, Kidderminster

The London Gazette reported the fact in great detail on 23rd August 1867 from information supplied by the Rt. Rev. Henry, Lord Bishop of Worcester, it read -"*The boundary is an 'imaginary line' from the boundary with Hagley to a point near Blakedown, in the middle of the Birmingham turn pike road, and extending thence southward for a distance of two and a half miles to a point opposite the boundary stone inscribed - K.St.G.D.C 1867, No1*".

The article continues describing a boundary line into town passing down the centre of Swan Street and into the Bull Ring; then over the Town Bridge before reaching the canal via Pitts Lane and the Sling cart way. The line then continued one mile down the canal towpath to Falling Sands Rolling Mill where it cut across to meet the boundary of the Parish of Stone.

A sketch showing the boundary of the parish can be found in the Appendix page 162.

The Rev. Charles John MacQueen Mottram MA - The first Vicar 1867-1872

The Rev. C.J.M Mottram had been Curate in Charge for the past fifteen years and it had been his job to represent the church at the various town meetings regarding the new parish and its boundaries. In 1867 he was confirmed as the first Vicar of the Parish of St.George, Kidderminster. Born in Scotland, he was a family man with a wife, Catherine, two sons and a daughter. His eldest son, also Charles, was a curate of the parish. In the 1871 census he is recorded as living with his family at the Vicarage in Hoo Lane with his servants.

City or Municipal Borough of	Municipal Ward of	Parliamentary Borough of	Local Board, or [Improvement Commissioners District] of	Ecclesiastical District of
Kidderminster	South	Kidderminster	Kidderminster	St. George

ROAD, STREET, &c., No. or NAME of HOUSE	NAME and Surname of each Person	RELATION to Head of Family	CONDITION	AGE of Males	AGE of Females	Rank, Profession, or OCCUPATION
	Charles J Mottram	Head	Mar	56		Vicar of St Georges Kidderminster ([illegible])
	Catherine Do	Wife	Do		62	
	Charles J Do	Son	Unm	32		Curate of St Georges Kidderminster
Hoo Lane	Henry G. Do	Do	Do	30		[illegible]
	Cordelia C Do	Daur	Do		23	
	Martha Taylor	Serv	Do		[illegible]	Ladys Maid Domestic
	Harriet Thomason	Do	Do		[illegible]	Cook Do
Do	Emma Do	Do	Do		[illegible]	Housemaid Do
	Edwin Rhodes	Do	Do	[illegible]		Groom Do

In total, he served the church for twenty years and when he died in March 1872, aged 57 years, he chose to be buried near to the church he loved. The photograph shows the location of his grave in the shadow of the tower [**CM** on graveyard plan later in the chapter on page 39]. His wife is also buried with him.

The stipends paid to ministers of the Church of England were not generally known but, in February 1868, the *London Gazette* disclosed that the stipend for St.George's new vicar was £140 per annum paid from the common fund in the control of Ecclesiastical Commissioners.

Church attendance

With the new parish system in place, the town and the church settled down to a period of relative stability. St.John's Church, built in 1842, was granted parish status at the same time as St.George's and it boasted 1250 seats.

The growth of the Church of England did not go unnoticed and the local newspapers followed the progress of church attendance with interest. The *Kidderminster Shuttle* reported that a census of the congregations on Sunday 13th November 1886 recorded that 1093 attended St.George's compared with 751 for St.Mary's and 582 at St.John's. It commented that 2792 souls selected the established church whereas 2559 chose nonconformity.

There were still eleven nonconformist churches in the town including Baxter, with an attendance of 644, New Meeting 416, the Salvation Army 380 and the Baptist Church 291. The Countess of Huntington's Church attracted 148 and the Bethesda New Connection 106. The Catholic Church had 308 worshippers on the day.

One of those who worshiped at St.George's was William Whitcomb.

William Whitcomb

William Whitcomb was born in May 1866 in a house on Arch Hill. His father was a weaver and it was inevitable that William would start his working life in the carpet industry. At the age of fourteen he joined Woodward Brothers in Church Street and then moved to Edward Hughes factory in Mill Street. He became involved with the Weavers' Union and was voted their president in 1909. For the majority of his life he lived in Baxter Avenue and was a regular parishioner at St.George's.

He married his wife, Amy, in St.George's and their daughter, Amy Victoria, was also christened in the church. In his retirement years he was appointed the People's Warden. However, William Whitcomb kept a diary and it was his daily record of town life that has provided the local historians with a feast of information. Extracts from the diary were published in a book prepared by George Hall in 1978. His close association with St.George's by location and attendance prompted many entries about church life - some are used in the following pages.
He died in Kidderminster General Hospital in 1960 aged 93.

P.S. At a meeting of the DCC in September 1990 it was reported that the late Amy Victoria Whitcomb had left a legacy of over £2,000 to the church. The money was to be spent on the fabric.

Burials - from the registers

With such a large new congregation and an extensive churchyard, St.George's became the place for a final resting place. The first St.George's Chapel Burial Register records the details of over 1500 burials during the first fifteen years.

For many years the church ran its own Burial Club to ease the financial burden.

The burial records make interesting reading and provide an insight into the social structure of the town at that time.

BURIALS in the Parish Church of St George's, Kidderminster, in the County of Worcester, in the Year 1903

Name	Abode	When Buried	Age	By whom the Ceremony was performed
Henry Charles Luton Ibait 5350	Infectious Hospital	February 23rd	4 Years	Theobald W Church Vicar
Frederick Walters 5351	Hoo Road	February 22nd	15 Years	Theobald W Church
Harold Walters 5352	Hoo Road	February 23rd	12 Years	Theobald W Church
Florence Ellen Shinton 5353	Findon Street	February 24th	28 Days	T. Fairfax Robson M
Emily Hill	Workhouse	March 3rd	72 Years	T. Fairfax Robson M

The home addresses of those who had died include Bird Lane [Hurcott Road], Love Lane [Offmore Road], The Closes [Baxter Avenue], Fish Street, Mount Pleasant, Lion Square, Carpet Hill [Hill Street], Holland Court [off Blackwell Street].

Most of these streets are shown on John Broadfield's 1859 map reproduced in Chapter 1 page 17.

The institutions recorded included the Infirmary, the Poor House, the Work House, the Fever Hospital and the "Infectious Hospital".

The Curate or Vicar of St.George's normally administered the burials. However, in the early years members of St.Mary's clergy also signed the register. A member of the Whittall family was buried in 1904 by "*a Roman Priest by Special Permission* ". Around the same time it was written "*This burial was certified under the Burial Law Amendment Act 43&44 Victoria by James Bennett* " who was the Parish Clerk.

Perhaps the most disturbing fact from the registers centres on the number of children who died in those times; they are listed as "*infants* ". One entry, dated 18th April 1874, records the burial of "*Body of female infant, name unknown - found in Oxford Street* ". Another entry with a tragic background "*A male person, name not known - found dead on the railway* ".

Adult life expectancy in the 1800s was also relatively low when compared with today. Death in the mid-to-late forties was common and few lived to be more than sixty years old.

Burials - the churchyard

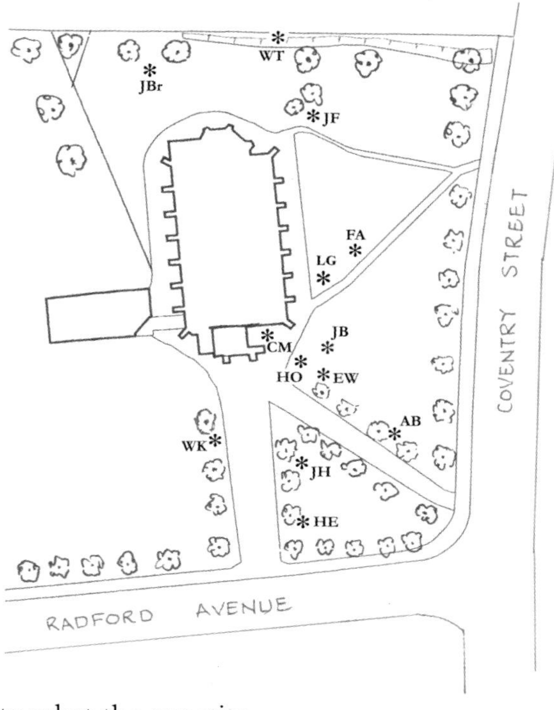

The three acres of churchyard today looks like others of the period with a jumble of headstones and graves in various states of repair. The majority are unattended and many are old and have unreadable inscriptions. In this day and age it is difficult to keep on top of the grass cutting and so, to the passer by, St.George's Churchyard often looks unkempt in appearance.

However, it is full of history and it is interesting to walk through and read some of the headstones. They contain the names of individuals who have played their part in church life and, perhaps more important, the history and development of the town. A complete review would become a book in itself - the following are a few examples to whet the appetite.

In the early 1860s a young John Brinton lived near St.George's at The Shrubbery with his second wife, four young children, two nursemaids, a cook and a housemaid. He was a partner in the town centre firm of Brinton & Lewis. In his private life he suffered a number of personal tragedies and in the eastern part of the churchyard, near the boundary wall, is a monument [**JBr**] in remembrance of his first wife, Anne. She died on 17th July 1863 aged 35 years and was buried at Monkstown in Ireland. They had three children and the body of their second daughter, Madeline Lucille, whom John referred to as "*the flower of the flock* ", is buried there. She died on her eighth birthday in an accident involving a model boat powered by methylated spirit. It appears that her crinoline dress caught fire and she suffered burns from which she died.

With his second wife, Mary, they started a family with the birth of a daughter, also called Mary, on 4th March 1866. She died one day later and is also buried in the grave.

Soon after this, John Brinton left the parish to live at Moor Hall in Stourport. He was a generous man and provided some financial help for improvements to the church - these are detailed later in the chapter. For the town he gave Brinton Park and also the Gothic Clock and Drinking Fountain at Worcester Cross. He was the town's Member of Parliament and later became a benefactor to St.Mary's where he is buried in a tomb near the church entrance.

In the early 1870s the churches of the town were becoming concerned about lack of space available for burials. St.Mary's closed its graveyard in 1872 and St.George's and St.John's had limited plots remaining. It was a town issue and the authorities decided to build a new public cemetery near the Nonconformists' Cemetery that had opened in 1843. The new Municipal Cemetery opened in 1878.

Although St.George's graveyard was probably the largest there were still 250 burials each year and something had to be done. Advice was sought from a local architect who was also a member of the congregation. His name was Joseph Thomas Meredith. A plot of land became available on the east side towards Elderfield House and an extension to the existing graveyard was considered. However, there were local objections on sanitary grounds and the project was stopped. The Parochial Church Committee remained concerned and advised members of the congregation to reserve their plots by contacting the Parish Clerk, Mr Bennett.

Hooman family tomb

There are many other stories of those buried in the churchyard. From the carpet industry the large square sandstone tomb that is so prominent to the right near the entrance to the porch is the final resting place for the Hooman Family [**HO**]. Although the majority of the wording is illegible, the name "Hooman" can still be read. Nearby, the graves of the Whittall family [**EW**] includes Eli who died in 1891. He was the father of Matthew who made his name in America and funded the Whittall Chapel in St.Mary's Church.

Thomas Edward Crane was buried in 1864. His company, Crane and Barton, built a splendid power loom mill on the riverside in Vicar Street. The upper part still exists and can be seen above the shop fronts.

James Humphries, founder of the Mill Street factory that became Carpet Trades, died and was buried in 1880 with his family in the west part of the churchyard near the driveway [**JH**].

John Brinton was said to have persuaded a French carpet designer called Alphonse Joannin Bouet to come and work in Kidderminster. He lived at "French Villa" on Comberton Road near the Chester Road intersection. He was a Sunday School teacher and died in 1887. His grave is situated close to the former main drive, on the right when approaching the church [**AB**].
Edward Hughes, the founder of a large carpet factory in Mill Street was buried in June 1902. He lived in Habberley Valley at the time and the diarist, William Whitcomb, a former employee, attended his funeral. Edward Hughes' Chief Engineer, William Youngjohns, died two years later and was also buried in the churchyard.
It is sad to relate that the location of many of these graves are unknown.

On a more general front Whitcomb also recalls attending the funeral of Mr A Gittins in September 1899 who was reportedly killed trying to board a moving tram. Local builder Henry Ankrett, who lived in a house he built in Comberton Terrace, was buried in 1869. His work can still be seen because he built many of the town's prestigious polychromatic [multi-coloured] brickwork buildings in the later half of the nineteenth century, typically Stour Vale Mill that was so close to the Worcester Cross School building. Henry Herring, another local builder who lived at Yew Tree House, was laid to rest in November 1904. His father started the business and was well known during the boom years of the mid to late 1800s.

The graves of those who served the Parish should not be forgotten including James Bennett who was "... *for 43 years Clerk of this Parish*." He died in 1904 aged 66 years [**JB**]. Other members of the Bennett family also held the office.

Joseph Thomas Meredith

Architect Joseph Thomas Meredith was a good supporter of the church and served on many of the committees particularly where his design skills could be utilised. His office and practice was centred in town at Bank Buildings, which was one of his earlier works. He is best remembered for his design of the Town Hall and Brinton's landmark offices in Exchange Street. In the late 1860s J.T Meredith needed all his skills as the church considered a number of improvements to the church's interior.

At his death, in August 1898, he had chosen to be buried with his parents and sisters in Rowley Regis. However, a private donor provided funds for a memorial window. At the time the committee were planning to remove the organ from the centre of the west gallery and in doing so, expose the triangular cusped window with three foils that looked down into the porch. This window was chosen and, in late 1898, Messrs Camm of Smethwick constructed a beautiful stained glass window using the theme of "*faith, hope and charity*". While there are no photographs of the memorial window, its location is discussed in Chapter 1 on page 21 and the window can also be seen in the photographs following the fire on page 70.

Chapter 4 The church's interior takes on a new look

East wall and chancel improvements

With the church now over forty years old, the formation of the Parish in 1867 provided the ideal opportunity to plan some improvements to the interior and the decor. A committee, led by the Rev. C.J.M Mottram contained some of the town's most influential people including architect J.T Meredith, carpet master Thomas Tempest Radford and wine merchant Charles Harvey. They considered a number of proposals that were eventually sanctioned following some generous donations from The Earl of Dudley and carpet Masters Thomas Lea, John Brinton, Henry Woodward and William Green.

c1874

Photography was in its infancy when the c1874 photograph opposite was taken. This is the earliest record of the church's interior. Taken from the west gallery it clearly shows the east wall following a programme of decoration undertaken in 1873. It provides the first opportunity to appreciate the grandeur of the church with its feature ceiling and rose window below. Observe the close packed horsebox pews; the angled gallery supported by the cast iron columns; the gallery seating and the Sanctuary door to the vestry.

The photograph below, taken some years later, contains more detail.

The furniture included an eagle lectern and clergy seats and desks presented by the Earl of Dudley, who lived at Witley Court. Carved from oak the seats displayed the coat-of-arms of the Diocese of Worcester. A new large octagonal pulpit also became a prominent feature. It was elevated and positioned in such a way as to give all members of the congregation eye contact with the preacher and an opportunity to hear what he said.

The 1873 improvements centred on a beautiful reredos behind the altar designed by J.T Meredith. It was described as depicting the "*Ascension in alto-relievo in the centre, with medallions on each side symbolical of the Four Evangelists* ". Carved by John Forsyth of Worcester it cost £600. A fuller description records "*A large panel formed with an arch supported by marble columns with decorated capitals surmounted by a gable with decorated mouldings between the arch and the gable. The panel contains figures sculptured in stone representing the Ascension of our Lord in the presence of the eleven apostles* ".
John Brinton provided some of the finance and it may have been his parting gift before he left the parish. The records suggest that the reredos was first installed in 1867 with some improvement during the 1873 programme.

The rest of the work involved an extensive decoration of the east wall and Sanctuary recess including the ceiling. The plasterwork was given a base colour before the addition of texts, patterns and medallions. The upper text read - "*HOLY HOLY HOLY LORD GOD ALMIGHTY WHICH WAS AND IS AND IS TO COME* " and at altar level, "*I AM THE VINE AND YE ARE THE BRANCHES* ".
The remaining decoration was credited to a Mr Preedy of London whose design was described as - "*A diaper on light ground with rich borders having eight medallions containing angels on blue ground. The lower ones being the four archangels Urial, Michael, Gabriel and Raphael painted in blue and gold paint* ". The four archangels can just be seen in the photograph to the left and right of the rose window.

In late August 1873 the church closed for four weeks as the craftsmen moved in to complete the work. Sunday services were held in the town's Music Room [Town Hall] and the beadles were charged with making sure the hymnbooks and kneeling hassocks were transferred and available for each service.

During this closure they also took the opportunity to clean and improve the vast ceiling with the addition of some grey tints that were designed to "*take away the bald and flat appearance* ". A bird's nest was discovered in one of the recesses!

The congregation would have been thrilled with what they saw at the reopening Harvest Festival Service. The ladies of the parish had produced a new altar cloth; new service books and offertory bags had been presented and the stairs to the pulpit had been carpeted with an "*ecclesiastical pattern* ". The Rev. F.R Evans, who had just taken over following the death of the Rev. Mottram, conducted the service.

One year later, in 1874, the church celebrated its Jubilee and it was decided to dedicate all the work to the memory of the first vicar of St.George's Church, the Rev. C.J.M Mottram, who had lived to see the fruits of his labours.
Later in the year the Rev. William Walsham How returned to St.George's to admire the improvements and preach at a Festival Jubilee Evensong.

The organ is replaced

The original Hill organ, positioned in the west gallery, was now over forty years old and in poor condition and funds were earmarked for a replacement. James Fitzgerald led a small team to agree a specification and place the order in 1869. However, it was not until the 1873 closure that the opportunity was taken to install the new William Hill three manual organ. Four years after it was again improved and enlarged by an organ builder from Birmingham called Mr Bossworth who commented - "*The instrument will now do justice to Mr Fitzgerald's skill* ". It should be remembered that church wind organs were hand blown with bellows. The organ blower had a very important job!
In those days it was normal for the choir to sit near the organ. They would probably not have been robed.

Church lighting

The inefficiency of the lighting has been discussed earlier and, over the years, the church committees would have considered the conversion to gas. The Kidderminster Gas Company first produced coal gas for the town centre streets in 1819 but it was some years later before a gas main was laid in the vicinity of St.George's. While the church records make no mention of the introduction of gas lighting the photograph shows what appear to be gas mantles on poles. The gas installation could have been part of the 1873 work or, perhaps, even earlier.

The Rev. Frederick Rawlins Evans MA - Vicar 1872-1876

Following the death of the Rev. C.J.M Mottram in 1872 the Rev. Frederick Rawlins Evans MA became Vicar. He was an educated man having gained his degree at Exeter College, Oxford. During his short term of office he endeared himself to the congregation to such an extent that when he left there were many individual presentations.

At his farewell service, in October 1876, the church was full and people even stood outside. He moved to become Rector of Bedworth and later became an Honorary Canon of Worcester Cathedral.

First Parish Magazine

January 1873

Parish life was busy for the new incumbent and there was a lot going on. The developing schools, the continuing improvement work to the church's interior and a full programme for the church organisations was often the subject of discussion and comment. And so, the Parochial Church Council decided to introduce a parish magazine so that all could share the news.
In those days printing was expensive but the town's newspapers the *Kidderminster Times* first printed in 1867 and, three years later, the *Kidderminster Shuttle* had led the way.

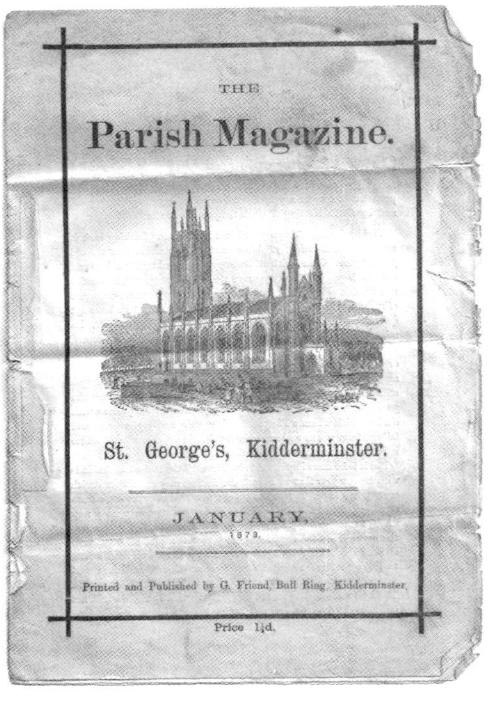

THE

Parish Magazine.

St. George's, Kidderminster.

JANUARY.

1873.

Printed and Published by G. Friend, Bull Ring, Kidderminster.

Price 1½d.

The vicar collaborated with publisher and printer G Friend, whose premises were in the Bull Ring, and the first issue of The Parish Magazine rolled off the press in January 1873 at a cost of one and a half old pennies.

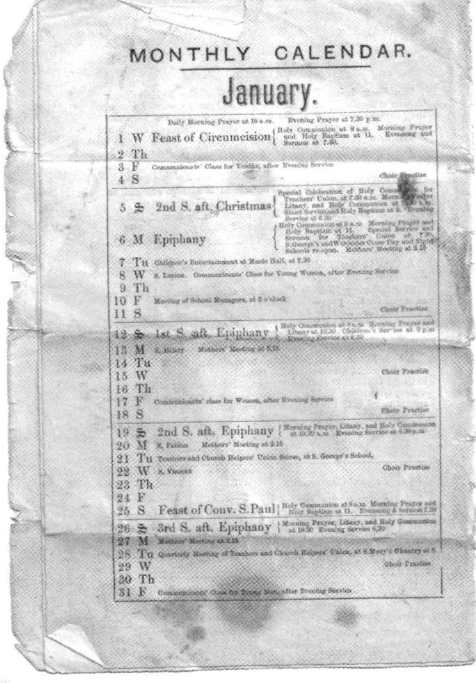

MONTHLY CALENDAR.

January.

Daily Morning Prayer at 10 a.m. Evening Prayer at 7.30 p.m.

1	W	Feast of Circumcision	Holy Communion at 8 a.m. Morning Prayer and Holy Baptism at 11. Evensong and Sermon at 7.30.
2	Th		
3	F	Communicants' Class for Youths, after Evening Service	
4	S		Choir Practise
5	S	2nd S. aft. Christmas	Special Celebration of Holy Communion for Teachers' Union, at 7.30 a.m. Morning Prayer Litany, and Holy Communion at 10.30 a.m. Short Service and Holy Baptism at 3. Evening Service at 6.30
6	M	Epiphany	Holy Communion at 8 a.m. Morning Prayer and Holy Baptism at 11. Special Service and Sermon for Teachers' Union at 7.30. S. George's and Worcester Cross Day and Night Schools re-open. Mothers' Meeting at 2.15
7	Tu	Children's Entertainment at Music Hall, at 7.30	
8	W	S. Lucian. Communicants' Class for Young Women, after Evening Service	
9	Th		
10	F	Meeting of School Managers, at 3 o'clock	
11	S		Choir Practise
12	S	1st S. aft. Epiphany	Holy Communion at 8 a.m. Morning Prayer and Litany at 10.30 Children's Service at 3 p.m. Evening Service at 6.30
13	M	S. Hilary Mothers' Meeting at 2.15	
14	Tu		
15	W		Choir Practise
16	Th		
17	F	Communicants' class for Women, after Evening Service	
18	S		Choir Practise
19	S	2nd S. aft. Epiphany	Morning Prayer, Litany, and Holy Communion at 10.30 a.m. Evening Service at 6.30 p.m.
20	M	S. Fabian Mothers' Meeting at 2.15	
21	Tu	Teachers and Church Helpers' Union Soiree, at S. George's School,	
22	W	S. Vincent	Choir Practise
23	Th		
24	F		
25	S	Feast of Conv. S. Paul	Holy Communion at 8 a.m. Morning Prayer and Holy Baptism at 11. Evensong & Sermon 7.30
26	S	3rd S. aft. Epiphany	Morning Prayer, Litany, and Holy Communion at 10.30 Evening Service 6.30
27	M	Mothers' Meeting at 2.15	
28	Tu	Quarterly Meeting of Teachers and Church Helpers' Union, at S. Mary's Chantry at 8.	
29	W		Choir Practise
30	Th		
31	F	Communicants' Class for Young Men, after Evening Service	

In the first issue the Rev. F.R Evans outlined the purpose of the magazine -" ... *the magazine will contain information on all matters of interest to the Parish; the Church, Offertory, Schools, Clubs, Accounts of all moneys given for Church purposes, Notices of Sermons, Classes, Meetings, Entertainments, and a register of Baptisms, Marriages and Deaths. .... with good and wholesome and instructive reading it will form a channel of communication between the clergy and parishioners, on matters hardly befitting the pulpit* ".

The first magazines resembled small booklets with the parish news on the two outer pages, front and rear. A bought-in pre-written centre section with stories and sermon-like articles, often accompanied by etched pictures, added value and made good reading. These were the days before commercially printed photographs and an etching was the established way to add a picture.

THE CRAFTSMEN OF THE BIBLE

VIEWED IN THE LIGHT OF THE MODERN EAST.

BY MADAME MUSTAFA BEN YÛSUF.

THE BAKER.

ONE of the first things that strikes you in an Eastern market-place is the row of bread-sellers ! Swarthy Arabs clad in white, twenty or thirty of them, squatting on the ground, with their large baskets before them. These are piled up with loaves, or rather cakes, of about seven inches in diameter and one or two inches thick. The bread is of two qualities, one fine and white ; the other coarse, brown, and heavy. They take a cake in one hand and with the other slap it vigorously, to draw attention to its size and quality, while they constantly cry, 'Buy, buy ! Who will buy the bread of life ?' even offering it you 'without price !' The bread is not bad, but owing to its not being enough baked becomes quickly hard and

9

It was noticeable that, whenever there was an appeal, the names of the benefactors were published together with the amount given, presumably designed to shame others into making a donation!

The magazine retained this format for a number of years despite the publishing company changing hands. In May 1875 it became Tovey & Elgood and in February 1878 William Hepworth.

Over the years the cost of production was a constant worry and income hardly balanced expenditure. In 1879 it was reported that the magazine was losing money despite sales of 450 copies per month. And so they took the bold decision to increase the cost to two pennies per copy. This caused a rumpus and the Vicar and Church Council considered ceasing publication altogether. But the demand was still there and so, after further discussions, it was agreed that from the January 1881 issue the cost would be one penny and a new magazine called "St.George's Parochial Illustrated Magazine" was launched with a slimmer addition called "The Dawn of the Day".

A complete set of the original news outer covers of the magazine is retained in the parish records at the County Records Office and there are a number of bound copies covering the late nineteenth century. Further copies can also be found in Kidderminster Library. They are complete and were compiled and edited by a Mr J.E Clarke.

The New Year.

WE cannot better begin the first number of S. GEORGE'S PARISH MAGAZINE, than by wishing all our readers and kind friends a very happy new year. We earnestly pray that it may be a year fruitful to all of much spiritual good, and by God's blessing of much temporal good also.

The beginning of a new year is a solemn time. Looking back it makes us think seriously. We cannot but remember that the old year is gone. Gone! with all its happinesses and troubles, joys and sorrows, hopes and fears, opportunities used or neglected, its service and its sins. For good or for evil it is gone never to return; no part of it can be recalled, nothing can be altered. And yet we have not quite done with it. The old year may be of use to us still. Its mistakes and failures and sins may teach us to avoid, in future, whatever led to them; and whatever success in the things of earth, or whatever progress in things spiritual has been granted to us, may beget thankfulness and gratitude to the Giver of all good, and stimulate us to further efforts and increased earnestness during the year that has now begun. Thus we part with the old year as with a friend with whom we have shared trouble and joy, success and failure, from whom we have gained valuable experience, and whose influence is therefore still felt, though he himself is gone.

But it is far more important to look forward than to look back. It is with the new year that we have to do. And we may enter upon it with courage and hope. The beginning of a new year is, as it were, a fresh starting point in the journey of life, it is the entrance upon a new stage in that journey, and it is well to start with a firm determination to profit by the experience of the past, to amend what has been amiss, to do better by God's help than we have ever done before, to make renewed attempts at self improvement, and more and greater efforts for the glory of God and the good of his people. To those who enter upon the new year in this spirit, it shall not fail to be, in the most real and lasting sense, a happy one,

THE MAGAZINE.

We are very grateful to the members of St. George's Congregation and other friends for the hearty welcome that has been accorded to the Magazine. The number of subscribers is already more than 500. No pains will be spared to make it useful and interesting. It will be recognized by some among us as an old friend with a new face, the central portions of its pages being those of a monthly periodical, edited by the Rev. J. Erskine Clarke, Vicar of Battersea, and extensievly circulated. The outer pages are published here and will contain information on all matters of interest to the Parish; the Church, Offertory, Schools, Clubs, Accounts of all moneys given for Church purposes, Notices of Sermons, Classes, Meetings, Entertainments, and a Register of Baptisms, Marriages and Deaths. The Magazine will thus combine useful local and especially parochial information with good wholesome and instructive reading, and form a channel of communication between the clergy and parishioners, on matters hardly befitting the pulpit. It is hoped that it may be also the means of promoting a still closer bond of unity between ministers and people, and of extending the interest felt in Church matters generally.

REPAIRS OF THE TOWER.

Every one interested in St. George's Church must be very glad that this most necessary work has been undertaken and completed, and that all proper precautions have been taken to prevent, as far as possible, any further damage from lightning, by putting up a lightning conductor.

The pinnacle that was struck and so much injured by lightning, last summer, was repaired at the expense of the Liverpool and London and Norwich Union Fire Insurance Companies, in whose offices the Church is insured. While this was being done, it was found that another pinnacle damaged some 30 years ago, in the same way, but more seriously, having been only patched up at the time, had become very unsafe and needed to be repaired at once. It was to enable this to be done as well as to pay for fixing a lightning conductor. that subscriptions were asked and so readily and kindly given. The tower is now externally in a state of thorough repair. There is still a Pinnaret on the South side of the Church, minus its top stone, which is some disfigurement to the uniformity of the architecture. It is to be hoped that it will soon be re-capitated.

The thanks of the congregation of St. George's, are due to the Churchwardens, Mr. B. Ankrett and Mr. John Knowles, by whose instrumentality chiefly the work has been carried out; also to Mr. Meredith, for kindly superintending in his capacity of architect without charge, and to all the subscribers.

More improvements to the decor

The improved appearance of the Sanctuary inspired others to make donations and these were introduced around 1876. A churchwarden, Mr Pearse, gave the carpet for the newly painted vestry and the vicar presented a chair. Thomas Tempest Radford supplied carpet for the side aisles and the nave but the main focus of attention returned to the east wall decor. This time it was the Rev. F.R Evans and his team who added some significant and colourful additions.

This photograph, taken at ground level after the completion of the work, gives a wider-angle view of the church. The black and white photograph does not do justice to the main improvement that saw the plain glass of the windows replaced with stained glass. The circular "rose window" received a floral design with angels bearing musical instruments. The two smaller windows near the outer walls giving light to the galleries were also fitted with stained glass. These depicted, on the north side, the "*parable of the ten virgins* " designed by Jones and Willis and on the south side "*the light of the world* " to a design by O'Conner. They were manufactured and installed by Thomas William Camm of Smethwick and were, in later years, dedicated to the memory of wine merchant Charles Harvey of whom it was said, he was "*a true son of the Church of England, who loved the place where God's honour dwelleth* ".

The photograph shows two large plaster panels of text that were mounted near the side windows. The northeast panel was headed "*Believe* " and, written below, the Lord's Prayer. The southeast "*Exodus Chap XX* " with the Ten Commandments below. Painted in red, black and gold these panels were also to a design by J.T Meredith.

The photograph also shows inscription texts painted on the arches over the north and south side windows. The exact introduction date and details remain unknown.

The Rev. Stephen Brown Bathe MA - Vicar 1876-1887

Stephen Brown Bathe was yet another Oxford Graduate who had studied at Balliol College. He had previously been the Vicar of Corley near Coventry before coming to St.George's in August 1876. He was in his early thirties and came with his wife, Sarah, family and servants to live at the Hoo Road Vicarage. Note: The lane had, by now, officially become a road.

The Rev. S.B Bathe also became very popular during his eleven years of ministry. It is clear that he took a special interest in people and this is emphasised by the fact that, in 1880, he trained 66 members of the congregation for confirmation by the Bishop of Worcester at a service on Palm Sunday held at St.Mary's Church. Perhaps it was this devotion to people and the organisations that led him to identify the need for a separate building in which to hold social events - more about this in the next chapter.

He suffered a long illness during his time at St.George's and, in the style of the day, on his return to active work in January 1879 he was presented with an Illuminated address that read - "*Dear Sir, We, the churchwardens and members of the congregation of St.George's desire to offer our warmest congratulations to you, upon your restoration to health, and the resumption of your work as Vicar of this Parish .... We are, Dear Sir, Yours faithfully* ".
There followed a long list of 250 names.

In 1887 he moved to the parish of Rushbury in Shropshire but died four years later. His popularity at St.George's manifested itself with the erection of a brass plaque to his memory.
Today , the plaque is still in place on the south wall of All Saints' Chapel, it reads -
"*To the Glory of God and in memory of Stephen Brown Bathe MA of Balliol College, Oxford. Rector of Rushbury, Salop. Who died on the fifth day of June 1891 aged 49 years. This tablet is erected in grateful recollection of his devoted pastoral work, unfailing kindness and ready sympathy with all in trouble while Vicar of this parish from October 1876 to July 1887* ".

The Organ and Choir are relocated

James Fitzgerald was involved in the planning of the next major reorganisation that saw the organ transferred from the west gallery to the ground floor in the northeast corner. The relocation, costing £506, was actually started in 1898 - two years after Fitsgerald's death.

The picture above, taken around 1900 from the ground floor, looks towards the east wall. The new location of the organ can be seen with the upper structure partly obscuring the text panel. It is apparent that some redecoration had taken place because the Sanctuary wall surrounding the rose window is now plain. Perhaps this was done to highlight the colours in the stained glass.

Note the area in the southeast corner and the location of the Rev. Bathe's memorial plaque which is to the right of the first window under the gallery on the south wall.

Not shown is the position of the font, which was near the west doors just at the start of the rear pew seating. Its mid-aisle position gave it pride of place.

With a need for the choir to be adjacent to the organ, choir stalls were added in a new layout of an enlarged chancel area that saw some of the front pews removed. A few of them would have been needed in the gallery where the organ once stood.

These details, and much more, can be seen on the photograph over the page. This postcard, issued as one of the *Valentines Series* was taken from the west gallery in the early 1900s and remains one of the best photographs of St.George's available.

ST. GEORGE'S CHURCH, KIDDERMINSTER
VALENTINES SERIES
35666

The 1800s - extracts from the Parish Magazines

In 1873 a group of ladies got together to make garments for the poor of the parish. They met at St.George's School in the evening and called themselves the "Dorcas Society" [to find out who Dorcas was, see Acts Chapter 9 verses 36-42]. Over the following years they worked hard and by August 1879 they had distributed over 1,000 items to the poor.

A number of clubs were organised by the church. These included a savings club called the Penny Bank Scheme, a Shoe Club and, perhaps the most ambitious, a Coal Club. Members of the club pooled their cash to buy coal at wholesale prices - sometimes a whole canal narrow boatload!

There was always a need for money and it was not unusual to hire the Music Room for special fund-raising evenings. On 24th November 1873 Mr Owen Maylott, of the parish committee, showed panoramic views of his tour of China projected by "*Oxyhydrogen Lime light apparatus on a disc* ".

The evil of drink was a good subject for discussion and so the church encouraged men to join the Church of England Temperance Society. They had an unusual oath - "*I hereby agree to abstain from the use of Alcoholic Liquor, except for religious purposes or under medical order* ".
A number of special Temperance Services were organised.

The church played its part as the town honoured one of the former preachers with the unveiling of Richard Baxter's Statue in the Bull Ring in July 1875. It was a civic occasion as the Dean of Westminster, Dr. Stoughton performed the unveiling.

Whit Monday was traditionally a day for the Sunday School Treat. After sports and games came entertainment by the school's Fife & Drum Band. A bumper feast at the Music Room followed with 1200 children sitting down to tea. 500 of the children came from the Sunday school and 700 from the day school.

The gas lighting was a vast improvement but for Sunday Evensong there was often a gas mains pressure problem affecting the intensity of light. The vicar agreed to write and complain to the Kidderminster Gas Company.

Mrs. Jeffrey became the first woman to join the parish clergy team in January 1877. She came from Durham and had experienced the hardships during a recent epidemic of smallpox. "*She will be visiting the sick and aged and reading them the scriptures* " announced the Rev. S.B Bathe.

Worcester Cathedral Choir Festivals were popular and a good opportunity to have a day out. Organist James Fitzgerald took twenty-five members of the choir to the Cathedral by train in July 1877. Arriving at Shrub Hill they walked to the Cathedral in time to join the other 1600 robed choristers for the morning practice. A bumper lunch was taken at the "Unicorn Inn" before returning to the cathedral for the late afternoon service. It was reported that the procession into the Cathedral was so long that the Bishop entered exactly twenty-seven minutes after the first choirboy.

Brinton's town centre carpet factory was part of parish life and when John Brinton built his gigantic steam engine, which he christened "Hercules", in 1879, he invited the Rev. S.B Bathe, together with representatives from the church to the official opening and the festivities that followed.

In the June 1880 issue it reported that new robes had been bought for the choir. A team of ladies made the white cotton surplices with material costing £12. 0s. 6d - all raised from donations. The old surplices were washed and sent to the new Infirmary in Mill Street to be cut up for bandages.

Problems were experienced in the tower and John Taylor's Bell Foundry was called in to help. From their 1882 register it reads "*re-hanging of three bells at St.George's in Kidderminster* ".

During 1884 the town was struck by two epidemics. Firstly, smallpox, which claimed ten lives, but by far the greater was the typhoid fever outbreak that followed. There were 1200 cases recorded in the town and 110 deaths registered. The Rev. S.B Bathe wrote an open letter in the *Shuttle* thanking all those who had made a donation for the sick in St.George's Parish. He commented that the recent anonymous donation of £18.14s.0d had been received and added to those given by others making a total of just over £40.

St. George's Parish room - George Street

In the 1887 edition of "*St.George's Almanack* ", which was actually written and published in 1886, the vicar appealed for funding to build a new "Parish Room". He reported that a piece of land had been donated in George Street near to the school. Finance became available and the plans were quickly drawn for a freestanding building with a large multi-purpose main room having a moveable partition allowing some storage. A small kitchen was added to the rear.

Things moved quickly and the foundation stone was laid on Wednesday 8th June 1887 and so the Parish Room was built. The much-needed venue soon became the meeting point for all the church organisations. It could also be hired privately for parties and social evenings.

8 June 1887 Foundation Stone of St George's Parish Room, George St, by Mrs Bathe wife of Vicar.

In more recent years the building of the Annexe adjacent to the church effectively replaced the Parish Room and so it was sold. It is now known as the Fred Bennett Centre, but it's sad to see the foundation plaque wording has been covered.

The old Parish room today

The building of the Parish Room was one of the last projects for the Rev. S.B Bathe before he moved to a new parish. His replacement was the aptly named the Rev. T.W Church who was to become the longest serving vicar of St.George's.

The Rev. Theobald William Church MA - Vicar 1887-1915

In 1887 Theobald William Church MA became Vicar at the age of 32 years. He was born in Devon and took his masters degree at Keble College, Oxford.

He had been a curate at St.Mary's and, in October 1887, when he transferred to St.George's, he was presented with the carved wooden chair that stands in the

Sanctuary to this day. Above the padded backrest is a brass plaque that reads - "*Presented to the Rev. Theobald W Church by the members of St.Mary's Young Men's Bible Class, October 1887* ".

During the years at St.Mary's he had cultivated a good association with St.George's because many of the burial records carry his signature.

With a sincere devotion to the church and the congregation he became part of the establishment for the next twenty-eight years. Like the previous vicars he lived at the Vicarage in Hoo Road with his wife, elderly mother and their servants.

When his ministry ended, on the last day of 1914, the church was in good order. He had been responsible for many of the major improvements and some of these were later dedicated to his name.

St. George's Vicarage, Hoo Road

In past years the Vicarage in Hoo Road had provided a good home for the incumbent of St.George's. But the Vicarage actually belonged to St.Mary's and in 1888, under the leadership of Rev. T.W Church, it was formally transferred. For the next forty years it remained the home of the Vicar of St.George's.

It was a large house with extensive grounds and it was described in a 1928 insurance survey, directed on behalf of the Worcester Diocesan Dilapidations Board, as the "*Parsonage House with stables and other outbuildings and enclosed stable yard with gardens, shrubbery and paddock. Total area being about three acres* ". The report valued the property at £3,035.

In a letter from the same board dated 23rd November 1932 it reported the Parsonage was "*sold and cancelled from the list* ".
The date coincides with the purchase of an alternative house nearer the Church that was to become the new Vicarage.
Full details in Chapter 8 page 91.

The Hoo Road Vicarage was subsequently sold and the area developed for housing prompting the creation of Vicarage Crescent in 1935.

The Vicarage today

A ride to Church

The Hoo Road Vicarage was more than a mile from the church and, in those days before the motorcar, the vicar and his family would have ridden to church in their horse drawn carriage.

There were a number of routes the carriage could have taken. The most direct would have been down Hoo Road, with its sloping close-packed new terraced housing and small shops, before passing the school and entering the Worcester Cross intersection.

Tree-lined Comberton Hill in the early 1900s. The Opera House is on the left.
Note: the shire horse drawn carts used to transport carpet to the railway station and the tram

Turning right, the carriage would have travelled up Comberton Hill past the Opera House before turning left into George Street. On the corner was the Swedenborgian Church.

Station Hill, as it was also called, was always busy with traffic to and from the railway station and following the introduction of trams, in 1898, the groom would have needed to be even more vigilant.

Travelling along George Street the Vicar could have admired the school buildings and the new Parish Room before turning right into Coventry Street and arriving at church.

While there are no records about this journey or any stabling at church it was probable that the carriages, and the grooms, waited in Radford Avenue.

Growing town and St. Andrew's Mission Church

By the late 1800s, and with a population of around 25,000, Kidderminster had changed its image. The factory system was firmly in place and the workforce received a fair wage. Children were given a good education from the improving church schools and the Land Societies were also busy building new terraced houses. Within the parish new street names such as George Street, South Street, Fair Street, East Street, Cross Street and Anchorfields had been added to the town map.

And so, the decision was made to build a small church to serve the community in this populated area. A site was chosen in South Street and work began with the construction of St.Andrew's Mission Church.

The church was financed and presented to the parish by the Rev. Clement Ernest Newcomb MA who was the senior curate of St.George's at the time. St.Andrew's became known locally as "*the tin church*" or "*the tin tabernacle*" because of its corrugated iron prefabricated construction.

Note : a similar church is maintained in the building collection at Avoncroft Museum.

Sketches by Muriel Robinson

With an interior lining of polished wood it cost £1,000 to build and could, remarkably, seat a congregation of 400 people. It was opened under licence on 24th January 1890. St.Andrew's soon became an integral part of the parish life and attracted a good congregation. It also boasted an organ, organist and robed choir.

It is evident that the congregation appreciated what the Rev. C.E Newcomb had done for the parish and they took every opportunity to prove the point. In August 1893 the Girls' Sunday School presented him with an "Illuminated Address" wishing him "*best wishes on his return home* " [from where we do not know]. It was signed by Eliza A Gardener, Clara Downton, Mary E Knowles and the Rev. Theobald W Church.

Some years later, when the Rev. Newcomb died, his funeral service was held in St.Andrew's Church on 17th November 1923. Diarist, William Whitcomb attended the funeral and wrote - "*There was a huge congregation and the service was very impressive. The Dean of Worcester read the lesson beautifully and the Vicar read the opening sentences. Canon Sladen and two curates were present also Mrs Newcomb who looked a pathetic figure on the arm of her son.* "
More about St.Andrew's in Chapter 9 on page 107.

Leswell Street School

With two thriving schools to its name a third was built in Leswell Street in 1899.
Leswell Street Church of England Infants School building still stands today - as photographs.

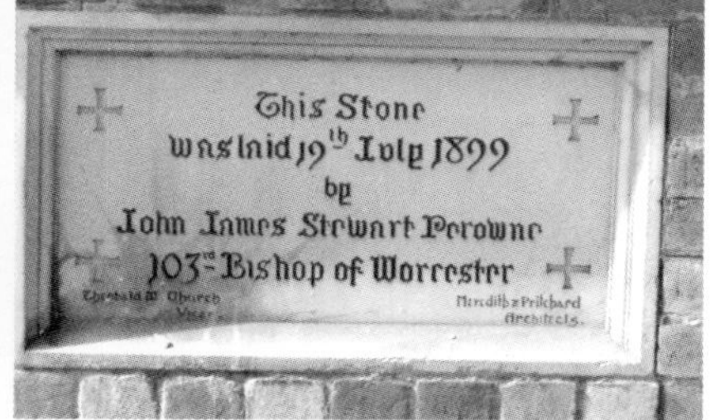

The prominent foundation stone remains and makes interesting reading. Built in the traditional school design by local architect J.T Meredith it repeats the feature gable end with the prominent cross and verse from the scriptures that reads - "*ONE LORD, ONE FAITH, ONE BAPTISM* ".

The depth of the church's involvement is uncertain but it is a fact that the Vicar and Churchwardens were appointed trustees under a covenant written in 1931.

More organists and choirmasters

James Fitzgerald's long reign came to an end in 1895 and the search for a replacement began. For a short time William Taylor, formerly organist at Wribbenhall, helped out before Edward M Chaundry MA. Mus.Bac., took the position. He lived in Park Lane.
Three years after his appointment he became involved with the transfer of the organ from the west gallery to the northeast corner.
Edward Chaundry remained for ten years until 1905 when William Taylor's son, Richard, was appointed. He was popular and presented the church with a signed picture entitled "*Christus in Gethsemane* " which hangs in the choir vestry to this day.
He lived in Lorne Street, was the Borough Organist and founded the Kidderminster Male Voice Choir in 1904. Richard Taylor FRCO was also a music teacher specialising in "*...Harmony, Organ, Piano and Violin* ".
After eleven years, in 1916, he left the town and was replaced by Henry William Radford who turned out to be one of the church's characters. Details later.

More about St. George's

Little is written about the members of the congregation who help out with the more menial tasks. The cleaners; the brass polishers; the gardeners; the organ blower and the man who attended the heating apparatus all played an important part in keeping the church looking and feeling its best. James Evans came into this category. He died in October 1878 and in his obituary it was reported that he had been the bell ringer for a considerable number of years. George Osbourne died in 1906 and they placed a plaque on the west wall close to the main entrance because for the previous forty years he had been the doorkeeper.

The gravediggers were also important but their workload was reduced in June 1910 when the Rev. T.W Church eventually closed the graveyard for burials "*except for burial in vaults and graves purchased before that date* ".

ST. GEORGE'S JUNR: BROTHERHOOD F.C. 1910 (I TEAM)

Sport played its part in church life. This photograph shows the football team of the Junior Brotherhood of 1910.
The team names were not recorded.

In September 1910 the Rev. T.W Church personally took on the task of making an inventory of the church's assets. In his own handwriting he recorded ...

* ***The Chancel*** - *2 chalices; 3 patens; 1 flagon; 1 large alms dish; Altar linen [items listed]; the Communion table; credence table; 3 Altar crosses; 3 Altar covers in red, white and purple; 2 chairs and desks; 1 carpet [Saxony];1 wooden procession cross and an American Organ.*

* ***The Nave*** - *Service books; clergy desks and choir stalls; the pulpit; lectern with lesson book; the three manual organ including fittings and a bench; the font with oak cover and brass ewer; two oak hymn boards; iron heating stove; bench and wooden chest containing 19 offertory bags and sundry towels; chest in south porch containing banner and fittings and in the porch near the west door - poor box and hymn boards. English Hymnals; Hymn and prayer books.*

* ***The Tower*** - *3 large bells, flagpole and flag; bench and other apparatus for funerals.*

* ***The Vestry*** - *Church registers; 1 oak table ink stand and pen; 1 large chair; 4 small chairs; 1 small font; alms box; book shelf with books; 2 mirrors; portrait of the Rev. William Villers; plan of seating; plan of church yard; fire place; coal box; fender; guard and accessories; surplice cupboard containing 16 boys and 16 men's cassocks and surplices.*

* ***The Safe*** - *Registers; communion plate; alms dish; large bible; communion vessels in basket; fire insurance policies; building and contents insurance policies.*

* ***For St.Andrew's*** - *Large bible; 3 alms dishes; insurance policies; books and old service registers.*

* ***Church Buildings*** *"St.Andrew's Church, St.George's School [mixed] George Street, Leswell Street Infants, Hoobrook Infants and the Parish Room.*

Hoobrook Infants - another St. George's School

Early records suggest that an Infants School was founded in Hoobrook in the mid 1800s. Its location was opposite the Crown Inn, near to the stream and behind the terraced cottages that bordered Worcester Road. Consisting of a single room it was administered by the parish of Stone.

The first mention in St.George's records comes in the November 1880 edition of the Parish Magazine when it is recorded that the Rev. J.K Key, curate of St.George's, took Evensong in the Hoobrook Schoolroom. Stone choir were in attendance together with "*many of the inhabitants of Stone and St.George's parish* ". It is possible that the photograph was taken in the schoolroom.

The village continued to grow and in 1885 it witnessed a major feat of civil engineering as the brick viaduct was constructed to replace the old wooden one. With the expansion came the need for a larger school and the discussions started.

However, it took time and it was not until 1912 that the foundation stone was laid for a new school building for 50 children nestling in the shadow of the railway embankment at the bottom of Hoo Road.

The old schoolroom remained in use by St.George's organisations until around 1960 when it was demolished at the same time as the cottages.

On the evening of Wednesday 10th April 1912, Mrs Rowland Hill, wife of the High Sheriff of Worcestershire, laid the foundation stone in the presence of Mr Rowland Hill and other family members; the Rev. T.W Church and the Rev. G.F Day, both of St.George's; Lady Cunningham; the Mayor of Kidderminster and other civic dignitaries; schoolmistress Mrs Johnson; builder George Law and architect Mr Pritchard.

The Rev. Church led a short service supported by the robed choir of St.George's with their choirmaster Mr Richard Taylor.

The Earl of Dudley donated the building site and Mr Rowland Hill and the Trustees of Stone provided part of the £500 building cost.
Rowland Hill was mayor of Kidderminster in 1907.

Staffordshire red brick formed the outer walls and the roof was of red tiles. On the gable end, engraved in stone, the words - "*ONE LORD, ONE FAITH, ONE BAPTISM* ".
In the grounds a well was sunk for the school's water supply. The building was completed in time for the return to school following the summer holidays.

A ledger entitled "*Hoobrook (St.George's School) Managers' Meeting Book - Kidderminster Foreign* " records the minutes of the early meetings of the school managers.
The first formal meeting was held at St.George's Parish Room on 5th September 1912 when the vicar, the Rev. T.W Church was appointed Foundation Chairman and Manager. A small committee consisting of George Law [the builder] Secretary, Thomas Greenwood, John Colley Tipper [Hoobrook Innkeeper] and Mr Harvey Silk representing the Worcestershire County Council Education Authority were present. The main business of the first meeting was the opening of the school and the handing over of the keys.

At further meetings, some held in George Law's Comberton Hill offices, the business of the school was discussed. Typical of the items recorded -

* Mr Silk reported that 36 infants were attending the school.
* Letters were exchanged with the Great Western Railway regarding damage to the well.
* Mr Law explained that a new sewage main pipe was passing through the area on its way to the town's pumping station and there was a possibility of making a connection.
* There seemed to be a continuous problem with the heating and the chimney flues with smoke blowing back into the classroom.

Subsequent vicars became chairman and the Rev. A.E.R Bedford was able to report, in 1916, that a grant of £90 had been received towards the general costs and "*Mr R Morris of Aggbro Farm had agreed to allow one of his men to act as sanitary cleaner* ". The school clock was beyond repair and the desks needed holes for the new inkwells!
In 1924 they were still having chimney problems and the vicar, by now the Rev. R.H Stephen, was asked to consult "*Mr Scott* ", the architect who was working on the new design for St.George's at the time.

The minutes also recorded the arrival and departure of a number of teachers at the day school who were all ladies. One Headmistress had been particularly active in her association with St.George's and the Hoobrook community. Her name was Cecilia Margaret Johnson and she lived locally at "Havenlea" opposite the Harriers' football ground. Cecilia Johnson became synonymous with the affairs of Hoobrook.

Hoobrook War Memorial

On 6th November 1920 the Hoobrook Memorial to those who served in the Great War was unveiled. It recorded the names of thirty-six villagers who fought together with Francis Perry who was killed in action. The Vicar of St.George's led the service and the unveiling ceremony was performed by Mr J Hill who was the son of the late Mr Rowland Hill. At a reception afterwards held in the old schoolroom opposite, Mrs Cecilia Johnson gave a vote of thanks. Today, the memorial stands in open ground on land where the cottages and old schoolroom once stood.

The First World War nears

During the First World War a number of the congregation fought for their country. Some lives were lost and their names are remembered in church to this day in the side chapel near the choir vestry.

At home, parish life continued but the needs of the church were not forgotten.
In 1914 a sub-committee was set up to consider improvements to the lighting. They suggested that the old gas mantles should be replaced by modern electricity "*if it could be afforded* ". They also commented on the inability of the old coal fired heating stove to warm the church.

However, the committee had other plans. These concerned modifications to the chancel area for the benefit of the growing choir. In 1916, after due consideration and careful planning, the pews under the gallery in the southeast corner were removed and the space enclosed by carved and panelled oak partitioning to form a proper choir vestry. A door was added in the east wall for direct access from outside.
The modifications cost £304 and were constructed under the direction of the architect Stanley Pritchard.

The original proposals had been the brainchild of the Rev. T.W Church who died on the 31st December 1914 before his dream had come to fruition and so it was decided to dedicate the vestry to his memory. On the 18th April 1916 Dr. Yeatman-Biggs, Lord Bishop of Worcester, performed the dedication ceremony.

Today, the former choir vestry is the location of All Saints' Chapel and the original entrance door location is concealed behind the chapel's altar curtain.

The Rev. Albert Edward Riland Bedford MA - Vicar 1915-1918

Following the death of the Rev. T.W Church, who was the longest serving vicar, the Rev. A.E.R Bedford was appointed and he turned out to be the shortest serving vicar staying for only three years. He was yet another Oxford graduate having studied at Brasenose College.

He left to become Rector of Morley in Derbyshire in 1918.

Henry William Radford - Organist and Choirmaster

During the early years of the Rev. Bedford's ministry a new organist was needed and, following a number of interviews, in 1916 Henry William Radford accepted the appointment as Organist and Choirmaster at a salary of £60 per annum. He bought a house in Roden Avenue and moved in with his wife and daughter who was also an accomplished organist.

He came with a good pedigree having been previously with St.Mary's, Morpeth in the northeast and before that, Assistant Organist at Winchester Cathedral.

After two years in office he became seriously ill and his daughter deputised for a while. She did well and received a letter of thanks and congratulation from the committee.

A new minister, the Rev. R.H Stephen, had been appointed and, over the following years, he received a number of disparaging remarks about the organist and the choir. The issue would not go away and things came to a head in March 1921 when the Parochial Church Council sat down to discuss a disturbing problem. Following complaints from the congregation and after due discussion, the Parish Clerk was instructed to formally write to Henry Radford making the following points -

1. *The choristers should observe the music's loud and soft passages.*
2. *Choir boys should be better behaved and needed more practice.*
3. *Mr Radford should not sing so loudly while playing the organ - "if at all!"*
4. *The responses should be unaccompanied.*

A written reply was requested and in it Radford said that he accepted the points raised, but suggested that to provide an extra night's practice for the boys his salary should be raised to £100 per annum!

There were others issues of concern, for example, it was noted that five adult members of the choir were still being paid for their services. It was suggested that other choirs in the area were completely voluntary and so the five were approached and subsequently agreed to forego their fees.

The Rev. Robert Hume Stephen BA - Vicar 1918-1932

The Rev. Robert Hume Stephen BA was another graduate of Brasenose College and he took over a thriving parish in a growing part of the town with a beautiful church in the best condition. He soon settled into the Hoo Road Vicarage at the start of his fourteen years as Vicar of St.George's.

After the First World War

The war had ended and brothers Harry, Godfrey and Jack Downton presented a new brass Altar Cross in thanksgiving for those who had returned safely from military service.

In later years a young Church Council member, Frank Ayers, became one of the choir's staunchest supporters and it was he who first proposed that the choir should be given an outing. This was agreed and, in September 1920, the first choir half-day outing went to Malvern by charabanc!
Frank Ayers lived in Shrubbery Street and eventually became the Parish Clerk.
He died in 1955 and is buried, with his wife, in the south churchyard near the pathway [**FA** on the graveyard plan in Chapter 3 page 39] .
More about Frank Ayers in "Hassocks & Cassocks".

Church finance

The church still attracted good congregations and with local support their finances were in good order. The Finance Committee met regularly and it was their job to apportion the money and control the expenditure. However, it was also their responsibility to make sure that the church and its contents were fully insured. The insurance cover was in the hands of the Ecclesiastical Insurance Company and, on the 26th February 1920, the committee considered and agreed a total valuation of £10,500 for an annual premium of £7.17s.6d.

Individual values - Church building £8,830; Seating and fittings £800; Organ £580 Bells £150; Stained Glass windows £140.

And so, in the early 1920s the Rev. R.H Stephen, from his Hoo Road vicarage study window, looked down on a town recovering from the war years. It was a time of prosperity and expansion but little did he know that his church would soon be writing the local front-page headlines.

The devastating fire of 20th November 1922

The country and the town had recovered from the war period and the carpet industry was again thriving. The town centre had good shopping with an excellent indoor Retail Market. The first houses built by the Borough Council had just been completed and there was a general air of stability and prosperity.

The St. George's team were also happy with the status quo. The fabric and decor of the church were in good order and they were starting to think about the centenary celebrations. And so, the vicar and the parishioners could not have been prepared for what was to happen in the early hours of Monday 20th November 1922.

St.George's Church - destroyed by fire

Sunday the 19th had been a busy day of services and all was reported to be well as the lighting was turned off and the large cast-iron heating stove near the west door damped down for the night.

The fire quickly took hold and the town experienced one of the most spectacular and devastating fires in its history. The church's prominent location, with its landmark tower visible from most parts of the town, together with the darkness of the night helped to make it even more spectacular.

THE KIDDERMINSTER SHUTTLE, SATURDAY NOVEMBER 25, 1922

St. GEORGE'S CHURCH.

Destroyed by Fire on Sunday Night.

AFTER THE FIRE

Residents in Kidderminster awoke on Monday morning to learn that in the night St. George's Church had been destroyed by fire, and that only the walls and tower of what was one of Kidderminster's landmarks had been gutted by the flames. At the close of the evening service on Sunday evening everything was apparently in safety.

How the fire originated is not clear, but it is surmised that it had its beginnings in the heating apparatus near the door which faces Radford Avenue, and immediately beneath the tower itself. What is known is that at about 2.20 on Monday morning P.C. Robinson

long period of 28 years, from 1887 to 1915. The church afforded 2,000 sittings, of which 1,700 were free. The living is a vicarage of the net yearly value of £593 with residence. It is in the gift of the vicar of Kidderminster, and has been held by the Rev. Robert Hume Stephen, B.A., since 1918, his immediate predecessor being the Rev. A. E. R. Bedford.

Many years ago the church was adorned with an altar piece embellished with a representation of the "Descent from the Cross," woven in carpet, with considerable brilliance of colour and elegance of design by Mr. Bowyer, a one-time manufacturer in the town; but this was wantonly cut in several places before

The fire started at the west end of the church, probably at the coal fired heating stove. The heater was old and had been the subject of recent correspondence between Mr H Cooke, the church's secretary, and local heating engineers H.E Pritchard & Sons. Unfortunately no work had been sanctioned or undertaken.

The Shuttle reported the event -

"*at 2.20am PC Robinson was on duty in Blackwell Street when he saw the flames. He ran to the town centre police station next to the Town Hall and reported to Sergeant Bint who rang the Fire Brigade. Captain W.M Hughes attended and assessed a need for help and summoned the Stourbridge Fire Brigade and their new 'motor fire engine' under the control of Chief Officer Walker. The local brigade tackled the blaze near the church and the Stourbridge brigade from Radford Avenue. PC Robinson informed the parish clerk, Mr Beech, who lived in Leswell Street and he quickly came down and opened the safe that was situated in the vestry at the rear [away from the source of the fire]. He, with the help of Sergeant Bint, PCs Moody, Short, Mason and Lowe was able to remove the offerings plate and the church register. By the time the Chief Constable, F Gray, Inspector Harris; the Vicar and the church wardens, Messrs Walker and Kettle, had arrived, flames were leaping 20 feet above the tower roof* ".

The interior of the church was totally destroyed. Two firemen, who were working in the choir vestry, were "*thrown to the floor* " when a supporting girder gave way. The Shuttle referred to the damage to the galleries, altar, reredos and bells and remarked "*not a semblance of the organ remained* ". It described the exposed brickwork and commented that the walls appeared stable but all the tablets together with the stained-glass windows had been destroyed. This included the memorial window to architect Joseph Thomas Meredith.

The reporter concluded his account - "*the church stands as a grim spectre, and not unlike many pictures to be seen of the devastated buildings in a war zone* ".

William Whitcomb wrote in his diary - "*We were awakened by a knocking on the door and Tom had come to call us. St.George's Church was on fire from end to end; it was an awful spectacle. The roof had eventually fallen in when we saw it at 3.30 am but the flames shot up sky high. I hurried off and in the Avenue at the bottom of St.George's Place the Stourbridge fire engine was at work and at the gates on the Coventry Street side our Kidderminster fire engine was at work. Not many people were about because the Bull* [Brinton's steam whistle town fire warning] *had not gone, so there was plenty of room, but nothing could be done to save the Church. The registers and plate was saved because the fire started at the belfry end. We could see and hear portions of the gallery falling to the floor from time to time. Water was poured on for hours, but when I went to work at 7.30 am the Stourbridge engine and men had gone leaving ours in charge. The Church is entirely burnt out; nothing remains except the Tower and the bare walls. We could see through the burnt out doorway a bell that had fallen. The flames were visible for miles around* ".

One of the survivors

Thompson's Photographic Stores

When it was safe to enter the ruins one of the first on the scene was William John Joseph Thompson who, with his wife Annie, were regular worshippers at St.George's. William was a well-known local photographer with a studio on Comberton [Station] Hill. His skill with the camera provided a perfect record in a collection of photographs taken at the time. Prints were sold to raise funds for the restoration and many are reproduced in this book.
It is possible that he also took some of the earlier pictures before the fire.
William Thompson died in 1928, aged 56 years, and is buried in the eastern part of the churchyard [**WT** on the graveyard plan in Chapter 3 page 39.]

THOMPSON'S

Photographic Stores

Kodak Specialists

EXPERT
in Developing Plates and Films.
Printing and Enlarging.

Practical Advice given to the Amateur and Advanced Worker.

PHOTOGRAPHY is OUR BUSINESS, not a side line.

Films left for developing during the day :: will be ready next morning. ::

39, STATION HILL,
KIDDERMINSTER.

In 1936 his wife presented the church with the beautiful Eagle Lectern to his memory. The Craftsman's Guild of London carved the lectern in a white oak similar to the organ gallery and the pulpit. The eagle stands on a pedestal with the figure of St.George and an English Rose to the front.

The lectern was similar to the one originally presented by the Earl of Dudley.

Damage through the lens of the camera

Aerial view

Looking west towards the tower

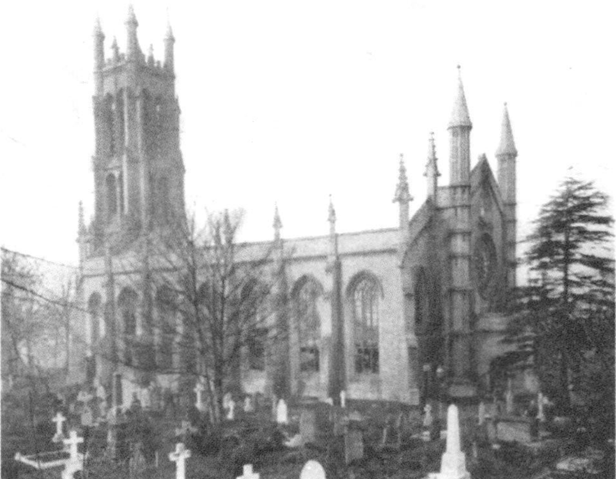
From Coventry Street, note the missing roof

Looking west towards main door, note the triangular window above which was the memorial to J.T Meredith

Looking west towards main door, note the cast-iron columns, the heating system to right of doorway and the central base of the Font.

Looking east towards altar, note the ceiling outline and the triangular window above rose window

Remains of the font

South wall and choir vestry, the Rev. Bathe memorial plaque survived the fire !

Looking south towards remains of choir vestry, note doorway in east wall and the memorial plaque on wall

Front entrance with firemen and a fallen bell

Remains of the Pulpit

Looking towards the main door, the heating stove is to the right

East wall, the reredos survived the fire

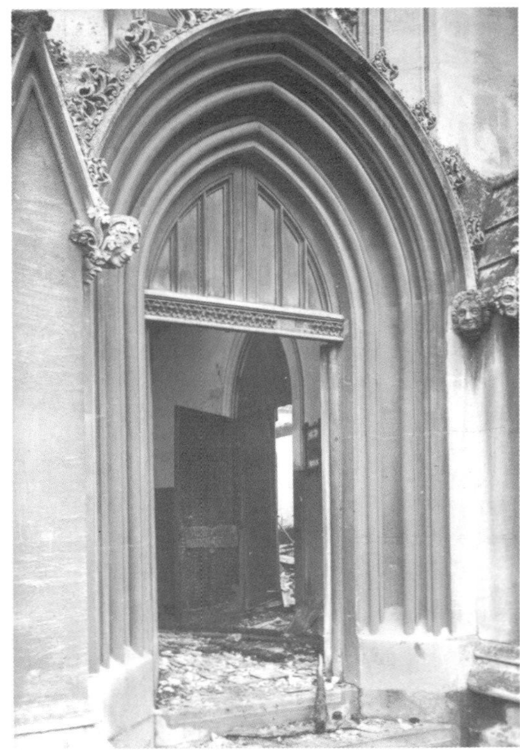

South entrance to gallery with doorway to nave

Meetings and temporary service arrangements

The Vicar and the Church Council called an emergency meeting to discuss the next course of action. They had received many communications offering support and help and so they decided to organise a town meeting in the Town Hall.

The vicar invited the Mayor, Councillor G.R Woodward a Director of Brintons Carpets, who was also an active member of the congregation, to take the Chair. On the platform were the Chairman; Canon Sladen representing St.Mary's; the Rev. R.H Bertie Roberts from St.John's and the Rev. R.H Stephen with the Churchwardens of St.George's.

The Town Hall was full as the Chairman welcomed everyone. He explained the depth of feeling that had been expressed in the many messages and letters received. He read out a letter from the Lord Bishop of Worcester before inviting Canon Sladen to address the meeting.

With the introductions over, the chairman presented a detailed report explaining the critical financial position. He confessed that the insurance valuation at £10,500 was totally inadequate to restore the building to its former glory and went on to explain that the architect Mr Giles Gilbert Scott had visited the remains and estimated a rebuild cost at nearer £18,000.

The shortfall was around £8,000, it was unanimously agreed that a special Restoration Committee should be set up to raise the money and oversee the rebuilding project.

G.R Woodward was confirmed as the first Chairman and Mr. A.B Banks of Hill Grove Crescent accepted the all-important job of Treasurer. Other members were elected and it was agreed that donations would be received by the committee or any of the town's three banks namely Lloyds, Barclays or The London Joint City and Midland Bank. The evening concluded with the vicar thanking everyone for their attendance.

The news quickly spread and individuals put pen to paper. The Bishop wrote in the *Worcester Diocesan Gazette* about the opportunity for "*a fine new church on the hillside restored and rejuvenated for the purpose of Divine Worship* ". A number of Letters to the Editor appeared in the next edition of the *Shuttle* commenting on the disaster. One started "*Cheer up St.George's - It's an ill wind that blows no good - now you have the chance for an even more beautiful church* ". A Mr. P.J Steward wrote from Witham in Essex saying he had made a wooden model of St.George's complete with organ, pulpit, seats and gallery and it took him fourteen months.

And so, with the Restoration Committee hard at work, the vicar turned his attention to the need to make alternative arrangements for Sunday worship. This was done and notices were circulated including a large advert in the *Shuttle*, which announced the following arrangements - *St.Andrew's Mission Church - Holy Communion 8.00 & 10.15 am; Matins & Sermon 11.00 am [choir please assemble at 10.45 am]; Senior Girls Class 3.00 pm; Evensong & Sermon 6.30 pm.*

In the Town Hall - Evensong & Sermon 6.30 pm [please bring your own Prayer and Hymn books]

The Restoration Fund

At the end of January 1923 the first donations list was published. Out of the total of £1,168 Brintons had given £300, G.R Woodward £250, Alderman Clement Dalley £50, George Randall [a chorister] £25, the Rev. Stephen £20, the Bishop of Worcester £5 and Mr. Frank Ayers £1. The sale of photographs by William Thompson raised £20 and other photographs taken by the Brown family added another £10 to the total.

On the 18th April a Grand Football Match was organised between Aston Villa and West Bromwich Albion. Played at Aggborough Stadium the game attracted 5,689. The Kidderminster Military Prize Band entertained before the game and at half-time.
Both teams were treated to a meal at the Black Horse Hotel with G.R Woodward acting as host. Each of the winning team received a rug woven at Bond Worth's carpet factory in Stourport. The match ball was sold for £8 and a total of £300 was banked. Unfortunately, there were no details of the match itself or the full-time score !

Many donations were received locally including some from street collections. Employees of the Matthew Whittall Carpet Company in Worcester, Massachusetts , sent $335 - they described themselves as "*former inhabitants of the old town* ".
Mrs Johnson put on an entertainments evening in Hoobrook and raised £5; the local branch of the National Union of Railwaymen contributed £4 and the Kidderminster Brotherhood [football team on page 60] collected £3. From industry Watsons Bros. and the Greatwich Spinning Company gave generously. Wine Merchants Charles Harvey & Company whose founders were members of the congregation sent £50.
All the donations were acknowledged in the weekly edition of the *Shuttle.*

In August 1923 the vicar presented an updated estimate of cost for the main items -

Rebuild [including heat and light]	*12,900*
Architects fees and expenses	*1,000*
Organ	*1,500*
Seating and fittings	*800*

By the end of the year the insurance settlement had been received and the bank account showed a healthy £15,000 - although still £3,000 short of the £18,000 target.

A Grand Bazaar

In 1924 the church was in its centenary year and so the vicar and his committee organised a Grand Bazaar to celebrate the event and raise money for the Restoration Fund. The Town Hall was the setting for a four-day extravaganza starting on 27th February. A programme of special events brought the crowds flocking in between 3.00 and 10.00 pm.

In the souvenir programme the vicar expressed his thanks to the other churches of the town for their support and made no apology for stressing the need to raise more funds for the restoration.
Each day patrons were treated to a classical music performance by a String Orchestra. There were concerts, plays and dance exhibitions organised by Miss May Fawcett.
In the Corn Exchange, a number of sideshows and "*games of chance* " giving the opportunity to win prizes - the "*star prize* " was a load of coal! An air of mystery surrounded the "*Character Reader's Tent* " with Mah-Jong from China inside, reading the palms and foretelling the future.

The Bazaar was a resounding success and so the vicar, G.R Woodward and his Restoration Committee breathed a sigh of relief and turned their attention to the next phase - the restoration programme for St.George's Church.

The Parish Magazine keeps people informed

With the rebuilding work scheduled to take over two years to complete the Parish Magazine became a vital part of the church's communications network. The front cover of the February 1925 issue retained the picture of the church before the fire but the rest of the text was devoted to keeping people updated.

FEBRUARY, 1925.

THE PARISH MAGAZINE.

ST. GEORGE'S, KIDDERMINSTER.

Clergy: VICAR, The REV. R. H. STEPHEN, M.A., The Vicarage, Hoo Road.
ASSISTANT CURATE, The REV. W. F. MALCOLM, B.A., 69 Shrubbery St., Kidderminster.
Churchwarden: MR. CECIL RHODES, 4 Batham Street.

Parochial Worker: MISS LIVESEY, 27, Lea Street, "At Home" Fridays, 6-8 p.m.
Organist and Choirmaster: MR. R. E. DAVIES, 47 Worcester Street.
Parish Nurse: MISS PETERS, 25 S. George's Terrace.
Parish Clerk: MR. H. BEECH, 33 Leswell Street.
Cases which the Clergy are asked to visit should be reported to the Vicar

HOURS OF DIVINE SERVICE:
St. ANDREW'S CHURCH.
Sundays.

Holy Communion 1st Sunday in month	7 a.m.
Every Sunday	8 a.m.
1st & 3rd Sundays in Month after Matins	11 a.m.
Matins	11 a.m.
Children's Service (3rd Sunday)	3 p.m.
Evensong	6.30 p.m.
HOLY DAYS.	
Holy Communion	11 a.m.
Evensong	4.30 p.m.

WEEK DAYS.
See Notice in the Church Porch.

Holy Baptism will be administered on Friday Evening at 7.30 p.m.: and on the 3rd Sunday in the month, at 3.45 p.m., *when Notice has been given to the Parish Clerk the day before.*

Churchings will be taken before any Service on Week-days or at other times by arrangement.

Choir Practice in the Parish Room at 8 p.m. on Fridays. The presence of any of the congregation will be welcome,

KIDDERMINSTER:
CHESHIRE & SONS, PRINTERS, COVENTRY STREET.

PRICE TWO PENCE.
(Published before the First Day of the Month.

Note: While the main contact point for parish business was the vicarage, the Parochial Worker, Miss Livesey of 27 Lea Street, was "*At Home* " on Friday nights between 6 - 8 pm!

Cheshire & Sons of Coventry Street printed the magazine. Price 2d.

Sir Giles Gilbert Scott. OM FRIBA 1880-1960

Giles Gilbert Scott was a Roman Catholic and came from a family of architects who lived in Sussex. In his formative years he was articled to architect Temple Lushington Moore. He quickly developed a flair for large buildings and in his early twenties was responsible for the design of Liverpool's Anglican Cathedral in 1903. This was just the starting point for a career that lasted to his death in 1960 when he was 79 years old.

Gilbert Scott was appointed President of the Royal Institute of British Architects in 1933. He designed many churches including one in South Africa but in stark contrast he is well remembered as the designer of the K2 Red Telephone Box that he first designed in the same year as the St.George's restoration project.
When he died he chose to be buried near the entrance to Liverpool Cathedral, but a service of requiem mass was said for him at St.James' Roman Catholic Church in London.

It is interesting to recall that William Knight, another architect, chose to be buried near St.George's and both men regarded the church buildings as their greatest achievement.

Gilbert Scott's vision

The Restoration Committee was reorganised and detailed to work with the architect whose offices were at Grey's Inn Square in London. Gilbert Scott was commissioned to prepare and present plans for the renovation of the outside and a completely new interior with seating for around 800. The cost was to remain broadly as estimated at £18,000.

He reported that, within the budget, there was very little that could be done to enhance the appearance of the outer structure other than make the necessary repairs. However, a thorough survey had confirmed that the body of the church was sound but there was a concern about the condition of the tower that had acted like a chimney during the fire. Some remedial work was specified.

He made a number of other recommendations.
For the churchyard he proposed the relaying of a proper path from the porch to the Coventry Street gate; the repair and re-hanging of the main gates; a new notice board facing the main road and a number of gas lamps to light the pathways.
Note : Although electricity was available gas street lighting was still the norm around the town and there was a main supply to the church.

Internally, he had a clean slate and this became the main focus of attention. He decided not to reinstate the galleries or the false ceiling but concentrate on the size and height of the building. His vision was a plain structure with two rows of Bath Stone pillars supporting a timber roof capped with tiles. The inside of the timber roof would be clearly visible from the nave.

This proposal excited the Rev. R.H Stephen and his committee and the plans were drawn for the church's lofty grandeur that exists to this day.

Building and specification

The original entrance doors were not reinstated and so a large open porch area under the tower formed the main entrance. Two sets of double doors, known as the west doors, gave access to the church itself. The two side doors in the north and south walls were remade and fitted but generally remained locked.

On entering through the west doors, there were two rows of pews on each side reserved for church officials and the sidesmen. Above this area was a short viewing gallery accessed from the tower stairway. The main body of the church and the sides were closely packed with pews fixed to the timber flooring. To maximise the capacity, the pews in the side aisles near the chancel were turned through ninety degrees. The pews were made of deal wood to a simple design and most of them remain in their original positions. The baptismal font was positioned at the rear of the south seating.

The aisle walkways retained the original stone but to help underfoot sheet-rubber flooring with the trade name "Ruboleum" was laid with two brown shades making the design. Note: Over the years the special flooring deteriorated and was ultimately covered by carpet.

The chancel area was increased in size and a new choir vestry built in the northeast corner. This location was directly opposite the former vestry that had been dedicated to the Rev. Church and it was decided to dedicate the new vestry to his memory also. The plaque over the doorway reads - " *To the Glory of God and in loving memory of Theobald William Church MA, Vicar of this Parish from July 1887 to December 1914.*
This choir vestry replaces the memorial vestry erected by Parishioners and Friends, which was destroyed by fire November 20th 1922 ".

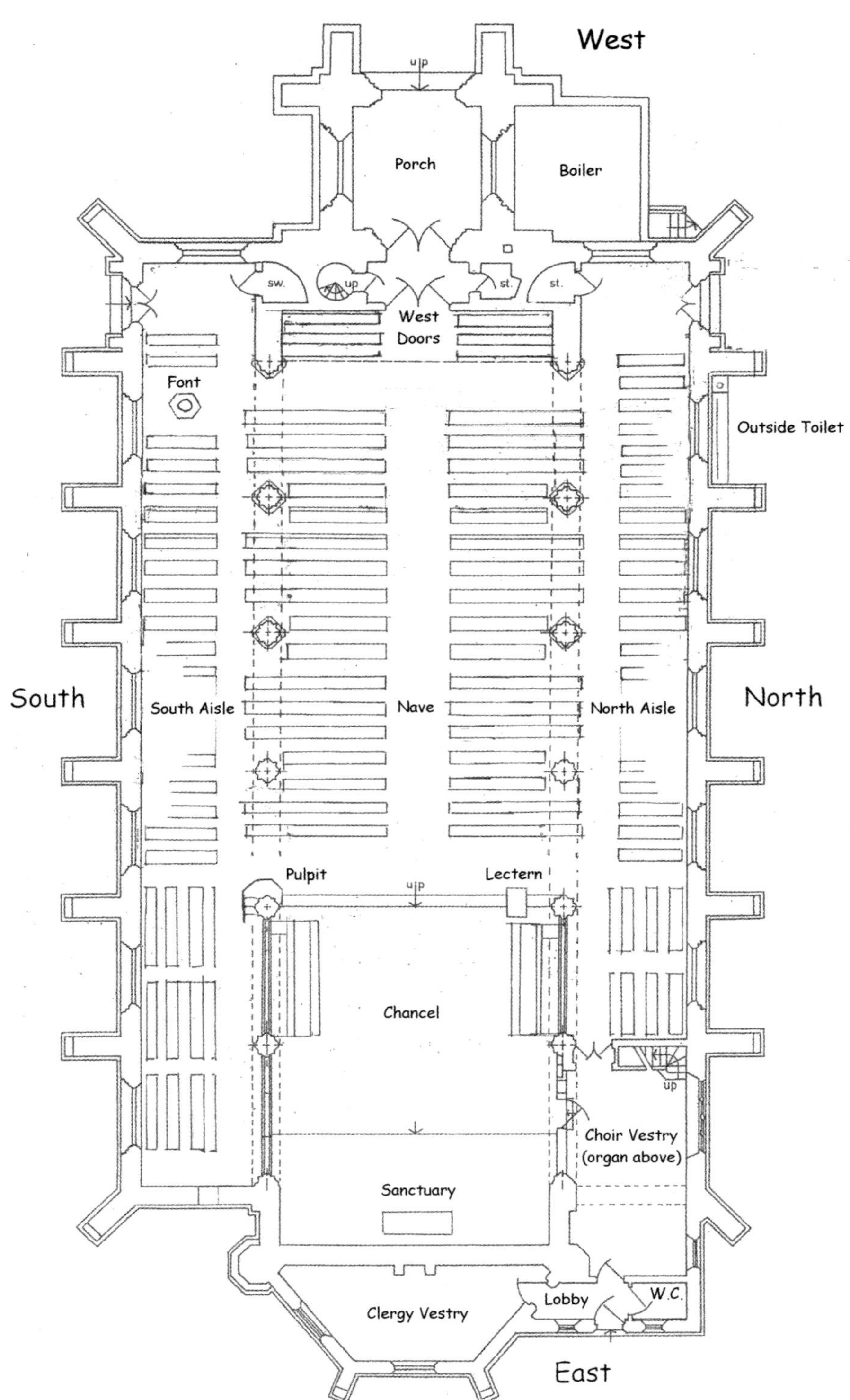

The drawing shows the internal layout of the church at the rededication

The drawing shows the layout of the chancel with two sets of choir stalls facing each other in traditional form. When facing the altar, those on the right-hand side are known as Decani and on the left side Cantori. These stalls are still in place and so is the segregated position at the nave end of the rear stalls. This special seat was for the Vicar who sat on Decani and his Senior Curate who sat on Cantori. Today they are used by the choir or visiting clergy.
The Craftsmen's Guild of London undertook the intricate wood carving of the altar, altar rail and the choir stalls.
Behind the altar hung a long dorsal curtain topped with a pelmet. The curtain was made from a dark blue material with a bordered pattern using gold.
The original door to the right of the altar was blocked up together with the outer entrance to the clergy vestry. A new external door feeding a lobby area with other doors to the clergy and choir vestries was added. A single toilet was also installed which was accessed from the lobby.
The plans for a new organ became a concern because the original Hill organ was completely underinsured. A subsequent appeal raised funds and a new two manual chamber organ, built by Nicholson of Worcester, was installed just in time for the rededication service. The organ was positioned above the choir vestry.
Heating and lighting used the latest technology with electric lighting installed at the pillars, pulpit and the lectern. The organ motor was powered by electricity for the first time.
The London company Rosser & Russell designed a heating system with large cast iron radiators fed by hot water originating from the new external boiler house on the west side of the tower. The boilers were coal fired and so, in colder months, the stoker charged the boilers on Fridays in readiness for the weekend services. The original boiler has gone but some of the large radiators are still in position.
The internal walls needed to be re-plastered and the cast iron window frames were repaired or replaced. The triangular window above the rose window was removed leaving the rose window as the main feature of the east wall. All the windows were glazed with a plain coloured leaded glass.
During the fire the three bells had fallen to the ground and were badly damaged. Having considered the state of the tower, the condition of the bells and the limited finance it was decided to install two new ones cast from the metal of the larger bell. Mears & Stainbank's bell foundry estimated the cost at £139 and was given the order.
The larger was 45 inches diameter and weighed 15 cwt. [0.75 Ton] and the smaller 18 inches diameter weighing 1 cwt. The inscription read - " *These two bells were cast from the original bell which fell from the tower of this church during the fire of 2nd November 1922. Mears & Stainbank 1924* ".

A beautiful carved oak pulpit was built to the design of Grinling Gibbons. Grinling Gibbons [1648-1721] was a well-known English wood carver who had been employed by Sir Christopher Wren to work on St.Paul's Cathedral.

A plain wooden elevated lectern and clergy desks and chairs completed the furniture.

Finally, a long list of fittings was added including hymn boards, cupboards in the vestry, umbrella stands and coat rails.

Churches in general always seem to have few toilet facilities and St.George's was no exception. The single vestry toilet was the only internal convenience. However, a flush toilet and a gentleman's urinal were positioned on the outside north wall in between the buttresses.

Restoration work

It took over two years to rebuild St.George's Church but, unfortunately, there are no detailed records or photographs of the construction work available in the archives. The architect would have appointed a local clerk-of-works to oversee the project but his name remains unknown. However, it is recorded that Messrs Collins & Godfrey was the main contractor and their site foreman was Mr Frederick Hopkin. Leading the team of stonemasons was Mr George Evans. The rest is left to the imagination with some help from William Whitcomb.

William Whitcomb visited the site in January 1923 and wrote - "*At the beginning of the New Year workmen have started to clear the debris. Today I had a look over the ruins. This is the first time I have been in the churchyard since the fire. The drive is in a terrible state, the wheels of the carts having cut the road up. Inside is a sad spectacle; nearly all the charred woodwork and twisted metalwork has been cleared away. To see a horse and cart up the middle aisle was a novelty, then looking up the Tower and seeing daylight right through shows the havoc wrought* ".
He also wrote in his diary that a short service was held in the shell of the church on the 22nd July following.

It is probable that the main construction work would have taken place in the body of the church leaving the churchyard and the graves clear except for access to the scaffolding around the outside.
One can visualise the piles of stone with the masons preparing each section before it was hoisted up to take its place. Imagine the new arches being manoeuvred into position without the mechanical aids of today!

When the masonry work was complete, the carpenters and joiners would have taken over preparing the roof structures at ground level before they were lifted into position. The carpenters had a lot to do before the tiles were laid and the rainwater gutters and down pipes installed.

With the roof watertight the internal fittings would have become the focus of attention. Plasterers working on the inside walls; plumbers installing boilers and radiators; the carpenters now preparing the floor and fixing the pews in position; organ builders desperately trying to keep things dry and clean; electricians running the conduit for the cables - and so on.
Finally, the all-important decorators closely followed by volunteers from the congregation who took on the job of cleaning the floors and polishing the woodwork.

Working in parallel with this activity was the necessary remedial work on the tower and the construction of new flooring levels, stairways and the installation of the two new bells. Whitcomb wrote on the 9th May 1924 that - "*the tower scaffolding has now reached the top and a small flag is flying on the south corner pole* ".

The Rededication - Sunday 13th September 1925

The Vicar and the committee closely followed the progress and, when the completion date was agreed, they started to plan the rededication service. The records explain that they enlisted the help of the Rev. R.G Parsons, Rector of Birch-in-Rusholme near Manchester who was able to advise with the formalities. He also preached at one of the services during the following week.

The first duty was to petition the Bishop, the Right Rev. Dr. Ernest Harold Pearce Litt.D, DD, CBE Lord Bishop of Worcester and he was presented with an illuminated petition prepared by Church Council member Mr Harry Deacon. It read -

"*Right Reverend Father in God, We the Vicar and Church Wardens, together with other members of the Parochial Church Council of the Parish of St.George, at Kidderminster within your Lordship's Diocese of Worcester do present this humble petition, that it may please your Lordship to proceed to the dedication of the building and furniture of our Parish Church now restored after destruction by fire* ".

With the Bishop's agreement the date was fixed to be exactly 101 years, to the day, after the Church's Consecration.

Photograph taken from the gallery 1930s
Note: carpet, Lectern and choir stalls

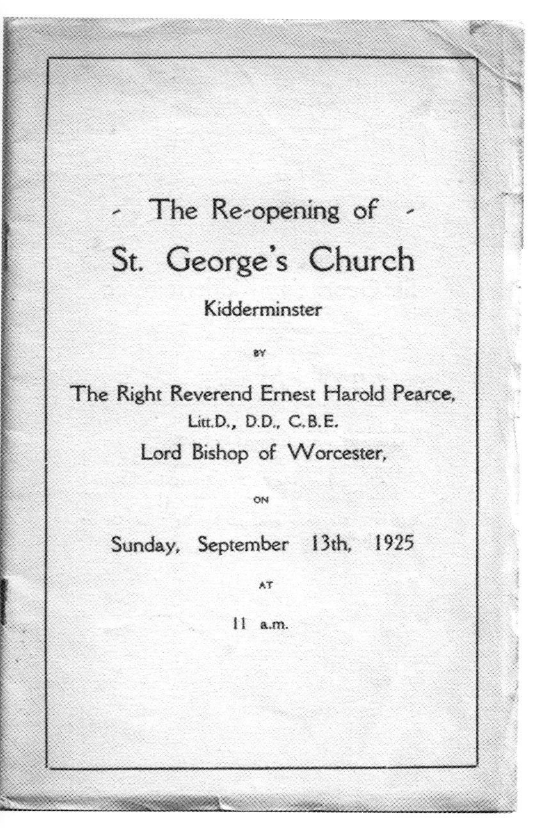
- The Re-opening of -
St. George's Church
Kidderminster
BY
The Right Reverend Ernest Harold Pearce,
Litt.D., D.D., C.B.E.
Lord Bishop of Worcester,
ON
Sunday, September 13th, 1925
AT
11 a.m.

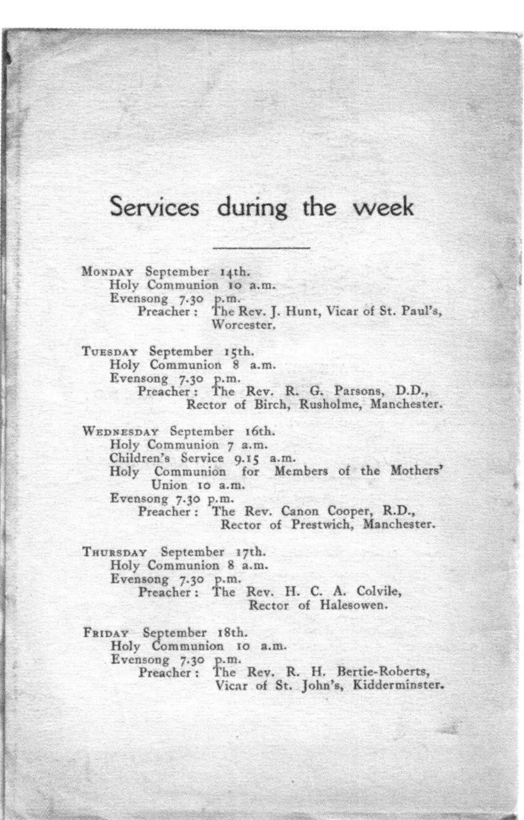
Services during the week

MONDAY September 14th.
Holy Communion 10 a.m.
Evensong 7.30 p.m.
Preacher: The Rev. J. Hunt, Vicar of St. Paul's, Worcester.

TUESDAY September 15th.
Holy Communion 8 a.m.
Evensong 7.30 p.m.
Preacher: The Rev. R. G. Parsons, D.D., Rector of Birch, Rusholme, Manchester.

WEDNESDAY September 16th.
Holy Communion 7 a.m.
Children's Service 9.15 a.m.
Holy Communion for Members of the Mothers' Union 10 a.m.
Evensong 7.30 p.m.
Preacher: The Rev. Canon Cooper, R.D., Rector of Prestwich, Manchester.

THURSDAY September 17th.
Holy Communion 8 a.m.
Evensong 7.30 p.m.
Preacher: The Rev. H. C. A. Colvile, Rector of Halesowen.

FRIDAY September 18th.
Holy Communion 10 a.m.
Evensong 7.30 p.m.
Preacher: The Rev. R. H. Bertie-Roberts, Vicar of St. John's, Kidderminster.

Four services were planned for the day with a separate programme for each.
At the 8.00am service the Bishop celebrated Holy Communion after dedicating the Holy Table. During communion Watts' famous hymn "O God our help in ages past" was sung.

At 11.00 am the establishment of the town were invited to a grand Civic Service with attendance by ticket only. The dignitaries, including the Mayor, Mr Cecil Brinton; members of the Town Council; Magistrates; Burgesses and representatives of other public bodies were requested to assemble at the Corn Exchange in the town centre at 10.30am. When fully robed they processed through the town to St.George's on what was described as a beautiful and warm September day.

At the church the civic procession was joined by the robed choir and the assembled clergy with the Rev. R.H Bertie Roberts representing St.John's; the Rev. G Crofts representing St.Mary's and the St.George's team consisting of the Rev. R.H Stephen, Vicar; the Rev. W.F Malcolm, Curate and Church Wardens H.C Rhodes and Joseph B.S Robinson.

The *Shuttle* reported that in church "*the sun picked out the crimson robes and jewelled chains* ".

The procession moved to the west door where, from without, the Bishop and his Chaplain, the Rev. Cuthbert Creighton, knocked three times on the door. On entering the Vicar's Warden Mr Robinson read the petition to the Bishop, who replied with the following salutation - "*Peace to this House and to all that worship in it; to those that enter it and to those that go out from thence* ".
The procession then moved on to the singing of Psalm 132 "Lord, remember David" stopping at the various stations for an act of rededication. These included the Font, Pulpit, Lectern, Chancel Steps and Sanctuary. The service proceeded with the singing of the hymn "City of God, how broad and far" before the Bishop preached his sermon. The offertory hymn was "O worship the King" and the party recessed to the singing of "Praise my soul the King of Heaven" at which point the civic party returned to the Corn Exchange where the Vicar thanked them for their attendance.

William Whitcomb was at the service and he commented that the church was full to capacity and the service lasted well over two hours! Also at the service were representatives of the construction team including Mr. Frankiss who represented Messrs. Colins & Godfrey the builders.

At 2.15 pm the Rev. Malcolm held a short service for the children.
At 3.00 pm the Rev. Stephen preached at a service for the regular congregation. During the sermon he commented on the changing scene in Kidderminster over the past 101 years. He referred to the fire and the generosity of the congregation and particularly former Mayor, Mr G.R Woodward, who had worked so hard with the Restoration Committee. He also commended Sir Giles Gilbert Scott and the builders for the quality of their work.

Evensong at 6.30 pm was another festival service with a sermon by the Venerable S.R James MA, CBE, Archdeacon of Dudley. He chose a text from the book Haggai "*The Glory of this latter house shall be greater than the former, saith the Lord* ".
He spoke about the new opportunities for the 9,000 souls that lived in the Parish and reported that he was pleased to see that the Parochial Register contained 1,100 names over the age of eighteen years who had been baptised. He went on to comment on the swing back to the Church of England from Non-conformity.

During the following week a series of 7.30 pm Guest Services brought sermons from the Rev. J Hunt, Dr. Parsons, the Rev. Canon Cooper, the Rev. H.C.A Colvile and on the Friday the popular Rev. R.H Bertie Roberts.

William Whitcomb's diary entry for the evening of the rededication sums up his thoughts - " *The church is fine now, noble in proportion and the lighting is excellent* ".

The Vicar reports in the Parish Magazine

While the local newspapers kept the town informed it was the monthly St.George's Parish Magazine that provided good value at 2d for the parishioners.
In the October 1925 issue an open letter from the Vicar said - "*My dear friends, I am writing during the week following the rededication of our church .....* " he went on to thank the many people involved but especially Miss Livesey who organised the band of ladies to clean the interior in readiness for the rededication service. He explained that the Vicar of St.Mary's, Canon Sladen, who was unable to attend, had agreed to preach at an evening service in the near future.
He spoke of the weather as "*a beautiful September day with not a cloud in the sky* ".

He reviewed all the services and finally thanked the Assistant Curate, the Rev. W.F Malcolm, who lived in Shrubbery Street; the Vicar's Warden Mr. Robinson; the Church Warden Mr. Cecil Rhodes of Batham Street and the Parochial Worker, the aforementioned Miss Livesey. He also thanked the Organist and Choirmaster Mr. R.E Davies, his choir, the Parish Clerk Mr. H Beech and the Parish Nurse Miss Peters.

With the pressure of the rededication over, St. George's could now return to normal parish life.

Lustreware

For some years a range of "Lustreware" was produced with a picture of St.George's church printed on the side. This small teapot was one of the set which also included the sugar bowl and milk jug.

Back to normal

After the excitement of the rededication, church life soon returned to normal as the congregation got used to their new surroundings. Although the church's interior looked very different, people soon appreciated and accepted the visual impact of Gilbert Scott's design.

The Sunday services were listed as follows -
"*Holy Communion, on 1st Sunday 7.00 am and every Sunday 8.00 am; Matins 11.00 am; Children's Service on 3rd Sunday at 3.00 pm; Evensong 6.30 pm.*
Holy Baptisms were conducted on Friday evenings at 7.30 pm in church and "churchings " were administered before any service or by private arrangement ".

The Parish Room continued to be the meeting place for most of the church activities. These included the Girls Club, Boys Brigade, Scouts and Guides, Mens Institute, Mothers Union, Young Wives, Young Peoples Fellowship and the Young Mens Club. Friday evening was reserved for choir practice and "*members of the congregation were welcome* ". The weekly Whist Drive was also popular.

Organists and Choirs

Little was written about the musical side of worship during the period of rebuilding. However, for the rededication there was a new organ, a comfortable vestry and some spacious choir stalls. New robes had been purchased and the choir reformed under the leadership of Robert Edward Davies.

The choir stalls today - Decani

In an earlier chapter the saga of William Henry Radford was related. He had crossed swords with the Parochial Church Council and at some time relinquished the position before handing over to Robert Davies. The exact date is not certain but it was a fact that Davies had been appointed in time to play for the rededication services. However, things were not working out for him either and his relationship with the church committee also deteriorated as they complained about the standard of music. In March 1926 he resigned.

Not for the first time the church now had to advertise the post and they were offering a salary of £50 per annum. One of the first applicants was a local man who came with a musical pedigree and he had all the qualities needed for St.George's. And so it was, that in 1926 a young organist and choirmaster was appointed who was to have a considerable influence on church life for the next 50 years. His name was Harold Evers.

Harold Evers - Organist & Choirmaster

Harold Evers came from a musical family. His father was the landlord of The Bird in Hand public house on the canal side near Stourport, but more importantly he was the leader and conductor of the Stourport Brass Band. Harold played the trombone but his real love was church music and playing the organ. He was taught piano by Isaac Wedley and later became assistant organist to J Irving Glover at All Saints Church in Wilden.

As a young man he played cricket for Wilden and football for Stourport Swifts. In the 1930s he was the resident pianist at The Opera House on Comberton Hill playing for the silent films. He was also an active Freemason, a member of the Vernon Lodge in Stourport and organist at the Provincial Grand Lodge of Mark Master Masons of Worcestershire.

During the First World War he served with the Band of the Worcestershire Regiment and saw active service in France at the battle of the Somme.

Note: Much has been written about Harold Evers particularly in Hassocks & Cassocks.

Problems with the new organ

With the false ceiling no longer in position, the volume of the church was now much larger than it was before the fire and it soon became evident that the new Nicholson organ was totally inadequate to support the singing of the choir and the congregation.

On the appointment of Harold Evers it was agreed that a new instrument should be considered. The Vicar, the Rev. R.H Stephen, sought the advice of a former colleague, the Rev. Noel Bonavia-Hunt, who had devised a tonal scheme that would provide plenty of power. Meetings ensued and an estimated cost at £1,300 was tabled for a necessary first phase. Church finances had not fully recovered and it was not until 1929 that the funds became available. The income came mainly from a number of generous donations and the proceeds from a concert given by the Stourport Brass Band.

Messrs G.H.C Foskett & Company of London was commissioned to manufacture and install a new organ in a basic two manual form with the provision for enlargement at a later date.

Stained glass window

The absence of any stained glass windows was a concern to many of the congregation. This was due to the shortfall in the insurance valuation. Individual members got together and launched an appeal and, by August 1928, over £250 had been collected.

It will be recalled that the two smaller windows in the east wall had previously been of stained glass. However, the organ pipes now hid the window nearest the north wall and so it was decided that the window near the south wall should be converted to stained glass once again.

Messrs Camm of Smethwick were commissioned to design and install the stained glass work.
It was described as follows-
"*In the tracery - Eve with Cain and Abel, the presentation in the temple, and Hannah and Samuel. The two lights - Virgin and Child, Elizabeth and John the Baptist* ".

A plaque under the window says -
"*The window above this plaque was erected in 1929 in Memory of Good Mothers* ".

The final cost was £267 and the Bishop of Worcester dedicated the window on Sunday 15th September 1929. Today, the dorsal curtain of All Saints' Chapel hides the plaque but the window has been one of church's treasures from that time.

George Richard Woodward

A stalwart of the congregation was Mr G.R Woodward who, as reported in a previous chapter, led the restoration team. He was the financial director of Brintons Carpets and in that capacity was responsible, with his fellow directors, for the donation of St.George's Park to the town.

In 1928, he made another generous donation to St.George's by clearing the church accounts of any remaining debts.
Dick Woodward, as he was known, was well respected in the community and had been Mayor of the town four times. He died while still in office and his funeral service was held at St.George's on 30th October 1934. It was a large civic occasion attended by the Earl of Dudley. The church paid its respects and the choir escorted the coffin to the church gates while singing the Nunc-Dimittis.
He was buried in Kidderminster Cemetery.

Processions, parades and exhibitions

In the April 1928 edition of the Parish Magazine the vicar announced that the Mayor of Kidderminster, Mr E.G [George] Eddy, had proposed the introduction of a "United Procession of Witness" for all the town's churches to take place on Whit Monday the 28th May 1928.
The vicar was enthusiastic and it was agreed that St.George's would play their part. And so, on a fine day in May over 3,000 scholars from twenty Sunday Schools of the town assembled at noon in the Bull Ring near Baxter Church.

The Mayor and his Chaplain, Canon Sladen, together with other civic dignitaries led the way followed by St.George's Sunday School at the head of the procession. The route wended its way around the town to the Corn Exchange where the band of the Salvation Army led the community hymn singing. It was a great success and became an annual event for many years to come.
In later processions St.George's church banner, held aloft by two senior choristers, led the procession closely followed by the robed choir and the Sunday Schools with the younger children riding in a lorry. It became St.George's tradition that the procession should be followed by the Sunday School party, often an open-air picnic with games.
Even with the reduced seating numbers St.George's was still the largest church in town, and it was adopted on the Sunday nearest St.George's Day as the gathering place for all the Scouts and Guides of the town. In those days before the ring road, a magnificent parade led by a number of marching bands brought the youth of the town together for their annual service. It was a colourful sight as the flags of the district lined the church drive. In church every conceivable space was taken as they packed in like sardines with the Cubs and Brownies sitting cross-legged on the floor. Finding a subject for a sermon that would keep everyone quiet and interested was a major problem. In later years one of the vicars used his imagination - all will be revealed in Chapter 11.
Today, things have changed and St.George's receives only the Cubs and Beavers.
In March 1931 Kidderminster Field Club held an exhibition of "Local Antiquities" in the Museum and Art Gallery in Market Street. Among the displays were "Relics from St.George's Church" comprising - the crown of one of the bells destroyed in the fire; molten lead from organ pipes; a glass bowl used for baptisms before the font had been installed and a medal commemorating the dedication of St.George's Chapel in 1824.

The Rev. Benjamin John Isaac - Vicar 1932-1945

In 1932 the Rev. R.H Stephen left the district and Benjamin John Isaac became vicar. At the time William Whitcomb was the People's Warden and he recalls that the Induction Service was well attended with a substantial collection.
Although the Rev. Isaac was devoted to St.George's and achieved a number of notable milestones during his ministry, it was a fact that he shared this love with service in the Territorial Army, which he had joined in 1915. This experience proved invaluable as the Second World War approached and in 1939 he enrolled for active service as Chaplain to 7th Battalion of the Worcestershire Regiment.

This effectively took him away from all church activities for the duration of the war.

When he first came to the parish in 1932, he took up residence at the Hoo Road Vicarage, but he was the last Vicar of St.George's to live there.

New Vicarage

From time to time the Diocesan authorities reviewed their properties and, in 1933, they decided to sell the Hoo Road Vicarage and its large and valuable plot of land. For St.George's they purchased a smaller detached house in Leswell Street.

The freehold property known as "Laurel Grove" was purchased from Mrs. Martha Ann Brown for £1,105. Although much smaller in size and acreage the new vicarage had the big advantage of being considerably nearer the church.

The deeds described the house as a brick building with a tiled roof comprising -

Inside - a drawing room, dining room, study, kitchen, cellar, five bedrooms, three lavatories [one outside], garage and wooden shed.

Outside - lawn and vegetable garden contained on three-quarters of an acre of land.

The Rev. B.J Isaac and his wife became the first occupants of St.George's Vicarage, Leswell Street.

St.George's Garden Fete

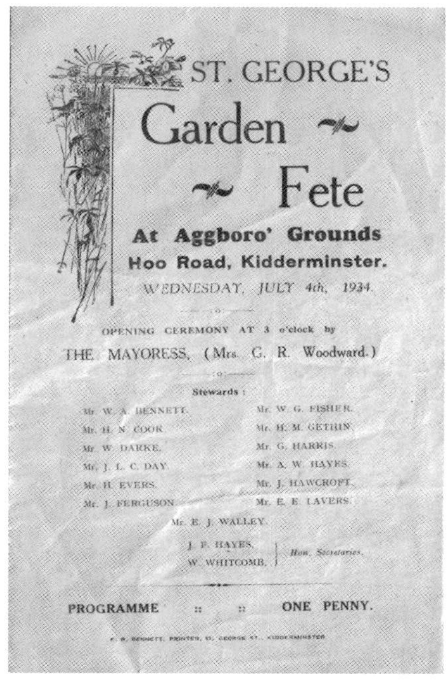

ST. GEORGE'S

Garden ~ ~ Fete

At Aggboro' Grounds

Hoo Road, Kidderminster.

WEDNESDAY, JULY 4th, 1934.

OPENING CEREMONY AT 3 o'clock by

THE MAYORESS, (Mrs. G. R. Woodward.)

Stewards :

Mr. W. A. BENNETT.	Mr. W. G. FISHER.
Mr. H. N. COOK.	Mr. H. M. GETHIN
Mr. W. DARKE.	Mr. G. HARRIS.
Mr. J. L. C. DAY.	Mr. A. W. HAYES.
Mr. H. EVERS.	Mr. J. HAWCROFT.
Mr. J. FERGUSON	Mr. E. E. LAVERS.

Mr. E. J. WALLEY.

J. F. HAYES, W. WHITCOMB, } *Hon. Secretaries.*

PROGRAMME :: :: ONE PENNY.

F. R. BENNETT, PRINTER, ST. GEORGE ST., KIDDERMINSTER

Over the years the extensive grounds of the Hoo Road Vicarage had provided an ideal setting for the annual garden party. However, the sale of the property created a problem for the committee. A solution was quickly found and the July 1934 Garden Fete was held at the "Aggboro' Grounds".

Note: It is likely that these were the open playing fields that existed on the right hand side when travelling towards Hoobrook. In the 1950s the fields became the home of a modern College of Further Education and more recently a housing development.

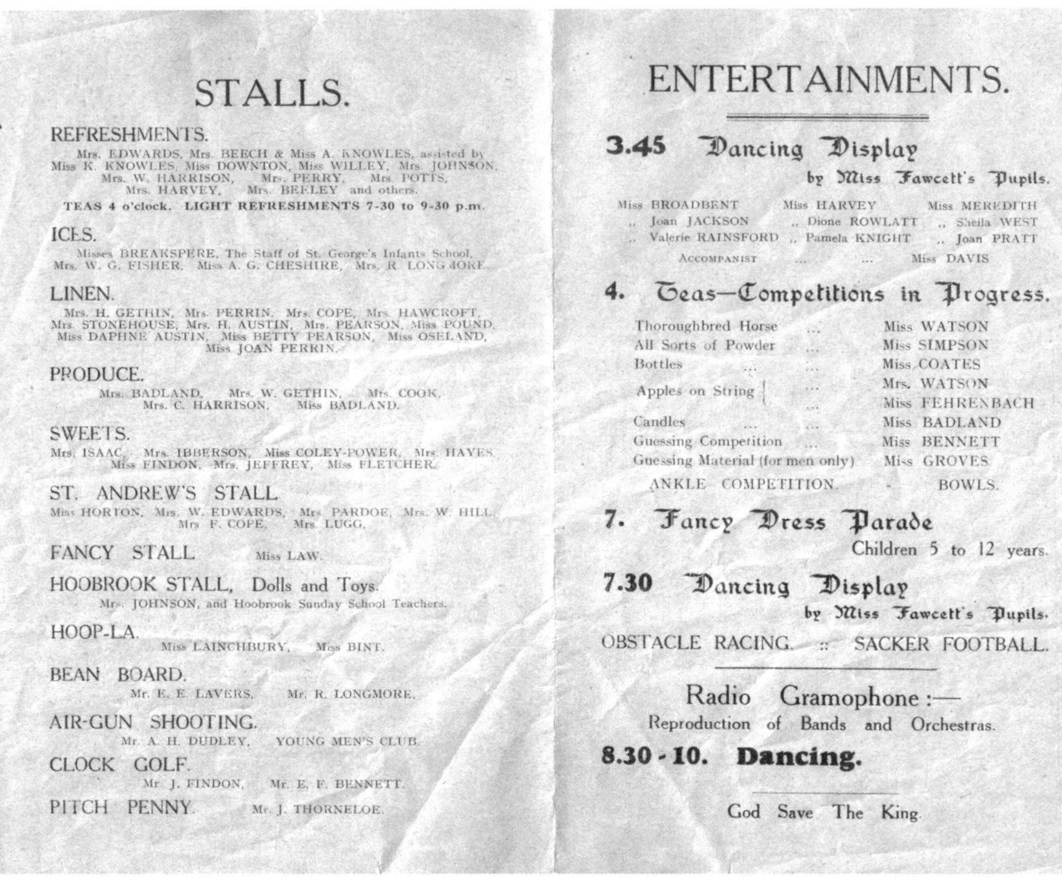

STALLS.

REFRESHMENTS.
Mrs. EDWARDS, Mrs. BEECH & Miss A. KNOWLES, assisted by Miss K. KNOWLES, Miss DOWNTON, Miss WILLEY, Mrs. JOHNSON, Mrs. W. HARRISON, Mrs. PERRY, Mrs. POTTS, Mrs. HARVEY, Mrs. BEELEY and others.
TEAS 4 o'clock. LIGHT REFRESHMENTS 7-30 to 9-30 p.m.

ICES.
Misses BREAKSPERE, The Staff of St. George's Infants School, Mrs. W. G. FISHER, Miss A. G. CHESHIRE, Mrs. R. LONGMORE.

LINEN.
Mrs. H. GETHIN, Mrs. PERRIN, Mrs. COPE, Mrs. HAWCROFT, Mrs. STONEHOUSE, Mrs. H. AUSTIN, Mrs. PEARSON, Miss POUND, Miss DAPHNE AUSTIN, Miss BETTY PEARSON, Miss OSELAND, Miss JOAN PERRIN.

PRODUCE.
Mrs. BADLAND, Mrs. W. GETHIN, Mrs. COOK, Mrs. C. HARRISON, Miss BADLAND.

SWEETS.
Mrs. ISAAC, Mrs. IBBERSON, Miss COLEY-POWER, Mrs. HAYES, Miss FINDON, Mrs. JEFFREY, Miss FLETCHER.

ST. ANDREW'S STALL.
Miss HORTON, Mrs. W. EDWARDS, Mrs. PARDOE, Mrs. W. HILL, Mrs F. COPE, Mrs. LUGG.

FANCY STALL. Miss LAW.

HOOBROOK STALL, Dolls and Toys.
Mrs. JOHNSON, and Hoobrook Sunday School Teachers.

HOOP-LA.
Miss LAINCHBURY, Miss BINT.

BEAN BOARD.
Mr. E. E. LAVERS, Mr. R. LONGMORE.

AIR-GUN SHOOTING.
Mr. A. H. DUDLEY, YOUNG MEN'S CLUB.

CLOCK GOLF.
Mr. J. FINDON, Mr. E. F. BENNETT.

PITCH PENNY. Mr. J. THORNELOE.

ENTERTAINMENTS.

3.45 Dancing Display
by Miss Fawcett's Pupils.

Miss BROADBENT	Miss HARVEY	Miss MEREDITH
,, Joan JACKSON	,, Dione ROWLATT	,, Sheila WEST
,, Valerie RAINSFORD	,, Pamela KNIGHT	,, Joan PRATT

ACCOMPANIST ... ... Miss DAVIS

4. Teas—Competitions in Progress.

Thoroughbred Horse ...	Miss WATSON
All Sorts of Powder ...	Miss SIMPSON
Bottles	Miss COATES
Apples on String ...	Mrs. WATSON
...	Miss FEHRENBACH
Candles	Miss BADLAND
Guessing Competition ...	Miss BENNETT
Guessing Material (for men only)	Miss GROVES

ANKLE COMPETITION. - BOWLS.

7. Fancy Dress Parade
Children 5 to 12 years.

7.30 Dancing Display
by Miss Fawcett's Pupils.

OBSTACLE RACING. :: SACKER FOOTBALL.

Radio Gramophone :—
Reproduction of Bands and Orchestras.

8.30 - 10. Dancing.

God Save The King.

The programme above gives all the information.
Dick Woodward's wife opened the Garden Fete and some of the names of the all male stewards are featured elsewhere in this book, particularly William Whitcomb and Harold Evers. Mr. E.E Lavers had a musical connection that is revealed in a later chapter and, at the time, he was the auditor of the church accounts.

The ladies played their part in the running of the various stalls. The vicar's wife helped with the sweets and Mrs Cecilia Johnson led the team on the Hoobrook Stall selling dolls and toys. Miss Fawcett and her pupils were again hired for the dancing display and the evening ended with ballroom dancing to music from a "Radio Gramophone".

Acoustics and improvements

The condition of the church tower continued to be a concern. In January 1933 steeplejacks M Macdonald & Co. installed a new lightning conductor and the local stonemason, George Brown, replaced a pinnacle for £14.

St.George's lofty proportions may have looked good but they continued to fuel the debate about the church's acoustic qualities. The new organ had helped with the music but the spoken word was now the subject of serious debate. In those days before microphones and amplification clear diction and often an exaggerated volume was needed to reach the rear pews. It was a major problem with no obvious solution.

Ten years after the rededication it was still an agenda item for the Parochial Church Council and they set up a special committee to research the matter and make recommendations. After a number of trials they reached the conclusion that there were two actions that would help.

The first involved the laying of a pile carpet. A large patterned square for the chancel between the choir stalls and a long runner from the chancel steps to the west doors was proposed. This suggestion had the bonus of improving the internal decor and so matching pew seating runners and a new altar rail kneeling strip was added to the order. The patterned carpet, based on a blue background in keeping with the altar curtain, was designed and woven at The Carpet Manufacturing Company in New Road. One of the church committee, Mr Eric Viney who was a director of the company, donated the carpet to the church. The carpet square can be seen in the photograph on page 82. Note : Although the main carpet has been replaced the pew seat runners are still in place.

The second proposal was more ambitious and involved the covering of the west wall with state-of-art "paxtile" sound absorbent tiles. A large area of these tiles is still visible today on the west wall over the gallery. During his lifetime Dick Woodward had been a supporter of this project and so his wife felt it fitting to provide half the installation cost.

In 1936 other donations were received. Mrs. Thompson donated the Eagle Lectern and local stonemasons A.W Brown Ltd crafted a new font. The font was carved from a Bath Stone to match the pillars of the church and given in memory of Mr & Mrs A.W Brown and their parents. See photograph on rear outside cover.

While these gifts were welcomed it should be recorded that permission had to be given by the Diocese before they could be accepted and used. In a deed issued by the Diocese of Worcester, dated 2nd April 1936, permission is granted, it states -

1. *Remove and burn the existing plain wooden font.*
   Remove the wooden Lectern to the Parish Room.
2. *Install Bath Stone Font.*
3. *Install new Lectern.*
4. *Improve the Acoustics.*

At a service on the 19th September 1936 Bishop Duppuy, former Bishop of Hong Kong performed the dedication. He was deputising for the Bishop of Worcester, Dr. A.W.T Perowne, who, at the last minute, was unable to attend.
The service was led by the vicar, the Rev. B.J Isaac assisted by his curate, the Rev. Noel Panter, and church wardens C.J Viney and T.R Badland. The choir sang the anthem "Lord I have loved the habitation of thy house" with a treble solo by Master Graham Scott. Graham's father, Bob, was the leading tenor on Cantori.

Harold Evers had now been the choirmaster for ten years and he had assembled one of the best all male choirs in the district and so he decided to take the first official choir and clergy photograph.

Choir photograph 1936

Front row seated - George Randall, Senior Chorister; C.J Viney, Warden; the Rev. B.J Isaac; Harold Evers; the Rev. Noel Panter; Thomas R Badland, Warden; Bob McFarlane, Senior Chorister.
Others - Harold Pritchard, back row second from left; Fred Buckley, second row from back extreme left; Leslie Guest, third from left; Bob Scott, fifth from left.
The gentlemen of the choir signed the back of this particular photograph.
Note: In the years following it became a tradition to take similar photographs with each new incumbent. These photographs are displayed in the choir vestry and a selection is reproduced in this book.

In this photograph the choir are wearing their new black cassocks and Whitney surplices - bought in 1927 for £21 - 10 shillings.

St. George's Yearbook

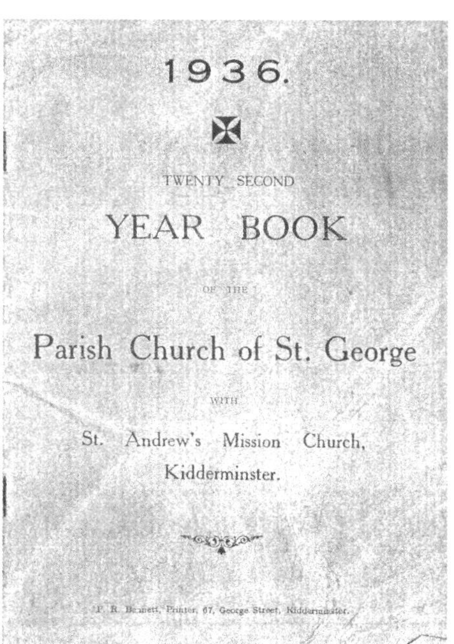
1936.

TWENTY SECOND

YEAR BOOK

OF THE

Parish Church of St. George

WITH

St. Andrew's Mission Church,
Kidderminster.

P. R. Bennett, Printer, 67, George Street, Kidderminster.

For some time the church accounts had been published annually. The 1936 edition is reproduced in full in the Appendix starting on page 157. This detailed account of church finances helps to paint a picture of parish life around that time.

Kidderminster is still a growing town

In the late 1930s Kidderminster, with a population of around 40,000, was still a booming carpet town although it was becoming common, in the autumn months, to see lorry loads of sugar-beet on their way to the new Sugar Factory on the Stourport Road. The town centre was a busy place with all the well-known shops and a fine market hall. The cattle market in Market Street on Tuesdays and the open air produce market on Thursdays maintained the feeling that Kidderminster was a typical "market town". Everyone knew the sound of Brinton's Bull as it bellowed the start and finish of the working day for the town centre's carpet industry. But the Bull was to have another use during the coming years because the country was on the verge of a war that was to influence the lives of everyone including the parishioners at St.George's Church.

Coventry Street School was a neighbour at the entrance to Radford Avenue. It was originally built in 1873 by The Kidderminster School Board for over 700 pupils.
It became a multi-purpose venue after the war and was eventually demolished making way for the Edward Parry Centre.

Chapter 9 Second World War and the post-war years

The Roll of Honour

At the start of the war some of the congregation were conscripted to the armed forces. The Rev. B.J Isaac became an army chaplain and many of the older members helped with the war effort by joining the Home Guard or working in the carpet factories that had been converted to the manufacture of munitions and armaments. William Whitcomb, although retired, worked at Carpet Trades in Mill Street making bullets.

St. George's remembers those who made the supreme sacrifice in two world wars with a Roll of Honour that remains in church for all to read. The Roll is retained in the Remembrance Chapel on the north side near the entrance to the choir vestry.
It has been the custom to read out the names on Remembrance Sunday.

L Crumpton	*C.V Edwards*	*Thomas Fidoe*	*N Harris*
Thomas Fr. Holden	*Thomas Norwood*	*Walter Denis Jones*	*Henry Martin Jones*
S.W Mills	*Thomas Mills*	*Samuel Newsome*	*Frederick W North*
Barry S Phipps	*Stanley Potts*	*Stanley Price*	*James R Spilsbury*
Isobel Squires	*George Stokes*	*George Sunderland*	*John Barrington Taft*
Clifford Warrington	*Thomas Wilkes*	*John Woodward*	*Malcolm Trull*

The individual personal and career details behind the names were not recorded but a search of the Burial Register found the death of Barry Seymour Phipps who was buried in the churchyard by the Rev. Isaac on 31st July 1945. Aged twenty-three, he lived at Holmwood on Comberton Road.
In contrast Thomas Holden died on 21st August 1944 when his ship was hit by two torpedoes from a German U Boat. In a moving ceremony on Remembrance Sunday 2006 his family presented a plaque and a picture of his war-ship, HMS Kite.

The absence of the vicar placed a greater workload on the assistant curate and this was a concern at head office. In May 1940, the Ecclesiastical Commissioners wrote, from their London Millbank office, a letter regarding the absence of the incumbent and the need to formally appoint a Curate in Charge. The letter recognised the special conditions of wartime and made a grant towards the stipend. Once again, St.George's had a Curate in Charge for those war years - his name was the Rev. Philip John Martin.

More about the Rev. B. John Isaac

When the Rev. B.J Isaac returned to civilian life after the war he decided not to return to St.George's, instead choosing to become Vicar of Wichenford near Martley. Although the reason is not formally recorded it could have been the fact that the Rev. P.J Martin had effectively run the parish during the five years of his absence and he had felt it only fair to him to leave the status quo.

Nevertheless, his distinguished war record should be recognised. In the early 1950s the *Malvern Gazette* published a report that seems to sum up the situation -
"*Rev. B.J Isaac MBE, TD, MA Vicar of Wichenford has been told by the War Office that he has been awarded 1st, 2nd & 3rd clasps to the Territorial Decoration. Mr Isaac was Chaplain to the 7th battalion of the Worcestershire Regiment for fifteen years until 1950 although his Territorial service dates from 1915. He is a former Vicar of St.George's Kidderminster, Minor Canon of Worcester Cathedral and Chaplain of Worcester Royal Infirmary and Newtown Hospital*".

The Rev. Philip John Martin MA - Curate & Vicar 1940-1959

Philip John Martin was educated at the Merchant Taylor's School in London before moving on to university at St.John's College Oxford. He was a bachelor and when he moved to Kidderminster, in 1940, he lived in lodgings in Shrubbery Street. For the next five years he guided the life of the parish through the turbulent war years. He was hard working, popular and well respected, walking everywhere in the performance of his parish duties.

In 1945 the Rev. P.J Martin formally became the vicar and moved into the Leswell Street Vicarage where he remained for the next fourteen years.

In 1959, after a total of 19 years devoted service to the parish, he married and moved to a new ministry at Longstock with Leckford in Hampshire. In later years he returned to this area with an association with St.Mary's at Oldswinford.

Michael Hale, in his book *Hassocks & Cassocks*, paints a good picture of the Rev. P.J Martin.

The War Years

During the war a national shortage of steel demanded the removal of the majority of the steel railings and gates from around the churchyard. The steel was reused for the manufacture of tanks and service vehicles. However, one section remains at the high-level east boundary with Elderfield Gardens. It seems remarkable that these substantial railings are over 180 years old. The origin railings and main gates can be seen in the photograph in Chapter 1 on page 22. After the war the missing railings and gates were not replaced.

Towards the end of the war, when some of the air-raid restrictions had been relaxed, number of public concerts were held in church performed by St.George's Chor Society under the leadership of Harold Evers who conducted the performances. Th Society consisted of the main choir augmented by other chorus members and soloist hired for the occasion. The Borough Organist, Harold Frampton FRCO, provided th music together with a small orchestra led by Mr Everard E Lavers.

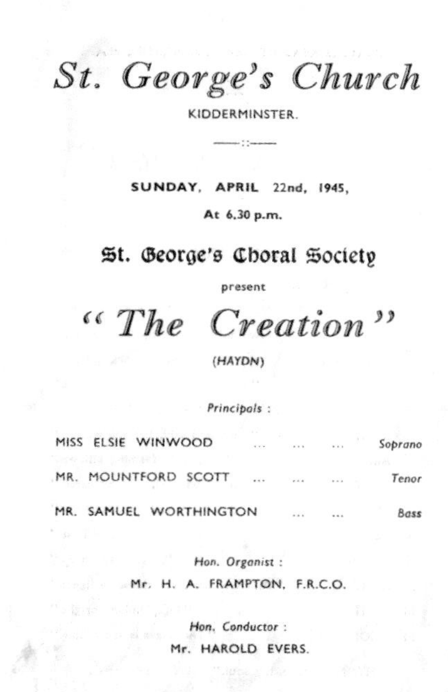

St. George's Church

KIDDERMINSTER.

SUNDAY, APRIL 22nd, 1945,

At 6.30 p.m.

St. George's Choral Society

present

"The Creation"

(HAYDN)

Principals :

MISS ELSIE WINWOOD ... ... *Soprano*

MR. MOUNTFORD SCOTT ... ... *Tenor*

MR. SAMUEL WORTHINGTON ... ... *Bass*

Hon. Organist :

Mr. H. A. FRAMPTON, F.R.C.O.

Hon. Conductor :

Mr. HAROLD EVERS.

The first concert, in April 1943, featured Handel "Messiah" with bass soloist George Pizzey c Westminster Abbey, tenor George Mountfor Scott of St.Paul's Cathedral and Mrs. L.V Southall, contralto, who was Harold Evers' siste In the following year Mendelssohn's "Elijah" wa performed in a packed church. The soloist wa Master Michael Evers, Harold's son.

With the war virtually over, the April 1945 concer featured Haydn's "Creation". The *Shuttle* reporte the attendance as being "*packed to the doors* ".

Author's note: As a young boy of seven years was my privilege to be a small part of th performance being the youngest member c Harold Evers' choir. I recall the principals, th men in tails and ladies in black evening dress. The chancel was packed to capacity with singer and the main body of the orchestra had to sit i the Sanctuary behind the altar rail - the "kettl drums" really took my eye!

The Royal School of Church Music

Most large churches had a robed choir in those days and the singing of church music was popular. In 1927 the School of English Church Music [SECM] was formed but in 1945, at the command of King George VI it was renamed the Royal School of Church Music [RSCM]. The aim of the RSCM was to promote church music and set a standard through the training of the affiliated choirs. St.George's was one of the early choirs to be enrolled on 1st June 1951. In the choir vestry is a framed copy of the enrolment certificate and the official coat-of-arms of the RSCM whose motto is -
"*Psallam spiritu et mente - I will sing with the spirit and the understanding also* "
By 1952 over 3,000 choirs were affiliated and by 1980 this had risen to 10,000.

Scheme of Music for June 1951

St. George's Parish Church

MUSIC FOR JUNE, 1951.

Trinity II. June 3rd.
Responses .. .. *Ferial* (R.S.C.M.)
Venite 3
Psalms .. .. M. 12 and 13 E. 16.
Te Deum .. .. CPC. 164 (Quadruple).
Benedictus .. .. CPC. 20.
Mag. & Nunc Dim. CPC. 247 and 14.
Anthem, " O come ye servants of the Lord " (*Tye*).
Hymns : M. 37, 512, 705.
E. 299, 16, 24.

Trinity III. June 10th.
Responses .. .. *Ferial.*
Venite 10
Psalms .. .. .. M. 19. E. 21.
Te Deum .. CPC. 241-242-243.
Benedictus .. .. CPC. 67.
Mag. & Nunc Dim. *Evers* and *Glover* MSS.
Anthem, " Holy art thou " (*Handel*).
Hymns : M. 4, 196, 211.
E. 297, 12, 31.

Trinity IV. June 17th.
Communion Service *Lloyd* in E flat.
Responses .. .. *Ferial.*
Psalm .. .. E. 24.
Mag. & Nunc Dim. CPC. 171 and 321.
Anthem, " Jesu, joy of man's desiring " (*Bach*).
Hymns : M. 321, 323, 318 N.D.
E. 522, 238, 477.

Trinity V. June 24th.
Responses .. .. *Ferial.*
Venite 24
Psalms .. .. .. M. 26. E. 29.
Te Deum .. .. CPC. 46-47-48.
Benedictus .. .. CPC. 185.
Mag. & Nunc Dim. *Wood* in E flat.
Anthem, " In humble faith " (*Garrett*).
Hymns : M. 5, 665, 657.
E. 260, 214, 274.

In 1951 the form of service was taken from the Book of Common Prayer. At the morning Matins service the Venite, Psalm, Te Deum and Benedictus were sung to chants selected from the Cathedral Psalter. At Evensong the Psalm, Magnificat and Nunc Dimittis were again from the Psalter or to a special setting. In those days the third Sunday morning service was reserved for a choral Holy Communion. Earlier Communion services were said. The hymns came from Hymns Ancient and Modern with the occasional hymn from the English Hymnal. An Anthem was always sung at Evensong. In October 1953 the new Parish Psalter replaced the Cathedral Psalter.

St. George's goes on the List !

The boom in manufacturing that followed the Second World War was a time of prosperity. New housing estates were planned in various parts of the town together with some modern blocks of flats. However, it was also a time to examine and preserve what had remained untouched by the bombing. St.George's Church had survived the war unscathed and in January 1953 the Church Commissioners, from their Westminster offices, looked at all the property in its care and decided that, under Section 30 of the Town & Country Planning Act, St.George's Church in Kidderminster was a - "*Building of Special Architectural and Historic Interest* ". In a letter to the vicar, the Rev. P.J Martin, the requirements were listed and it clearly stated that - "*If the building ceases to be used for ecclesiastical purposes it will be an offence to demolish it or alter or extend it in such a way as to seriously affect its character* ". In 1973 the church building was given the listing classification Grade 2* [Building of particular importance] by English Heritage and the authorities.
Perhaps the most outstanding feature of the church is the tower that can be seen from most parts of the town and surrounding countryside. The Borough of Kidderminster realised this in June 1953 when they chose to help celebrate the Coronation of Her Majesty Queen Elizabeth II by lighting up the tower with some powerful floodlights.

Ye. Stoure Vale Archers a shootynge for ye Pryzes.

One of the town's treasures is the 1850 painting opposite of "Ye Stour Vale Archers" as they practice at Whitville on the other side of town - even on this early picture St.George's tower is clearly visible !

Views from the top of the tower are equally spectacular as can be seen in the 1950s photograph that shows the park and captures the town centre with the prominent Slingfield Mill and gasholders before they were demolished.
Note: On the front cover the church can be seen at its best when viewed from the tower of St.Mary's church.

All Saints' Chapel

It will be recalled that the southeast corner of the church was, before the fire, the location of the first choir vestry with its entry door in the east wall directly under the stained glass window. For many years this door had not been used and so the area was selected as the location for a new side chapel.
In 1949 Kidderminster's Borough Surveyor, Harold Frampton, was asked to prepare some sketches. However, it was not until some years later that the new All Saints' Chapel was named and dedicated. It was also affectionately known as "The Lady Chapel" because of the stained glass window above dedicated to Good Mothers.

A small committee was formed consisting of the vicar, diocesan reader Leslie Guest together with churchwardens Basil Gethin and Victor [Vic] Summers. They considered Frampton's sketches and discussed the details with Sir Giles Gilbert Scott.

A plan was eventually agreed and the drawings issued. Local builders C & L Walker Ltd. were contracted to do the work. A Communion Table, carved from English oak, was ordered from Messrs J.L Green & Vardy Ltd. They also provided the oak communion rails. The existing pew seating was turned around to face the east. A new dorsal curtain behind the Communion Table hid the redundant doorway. The altar table furniture consisted of a carved wooden cross with flower vases painted in antique silver and ebonised.

All Saints' Chapel was dedicated on Sunday 17th March 1957.
The service, starting at 3.00 pm, was led by the vicar, the Rev. P.J Martin, with the act of dedication performed by the Right Rev. Dr. Lewis Mervyn Charles Edwards Lord Bishop of Worcester who also preached the Sermon. During the service Leslie Guest, who had worked so hard to bring the project to fruition, read a lesson.

After the sermon William Walsham How's great hymn "For All the Saints" was sung and in the service programme it was recorded -
"*At a service on 19th November 1848 the preacher was the Rev. W.W How who ministered at St.George's between 1846 and 1848. This appears to be the last sermon preached by the future Bishop and Hymn-writer during his ministry at St.George's* ".

A red Commemoration Book listed the names of 24 people "*by whom, and in whose memory* " the chapel was built, principally the Fehrenbach family who, for many years, owned a High Street confectionary shop and tea rooms.

Leslie Guest and family connections

Leslie Leonard Guest [1915-2002] was a good servant to the church and served in a variety of ways for many years. In Chapter 8 he can be seen as a member of choir, he was the Superintendent of the Sunday School and for twenty-five years he was one of the parish Licensed Readers.
In 1963 he was ordained to the ministry and, following a short curacy at Malvern Christ Church, he became the Vicar of Norton and Lenchwick. Other appointments followed and when he retired, in 1984, he chose to return and live in the parish near his family.
He died in 2002 and is buried in the churchyard [**LG** on the churchyard plan in Chapter 3 page 39]. The Guest family, wife Laura and son Tim were core members of the church. Another family falling into the same category was the Summers family led by church warden Vic Summers. He was married to Vera, an accomplished musician, who for a number of years was assistant organist to Harold Evers. These two families were linked when son Tim Guest married daughter Peggy Summers.

One of the many committees that Leslie served on was the CMS committee.

Church Missionary Society

St.George's congregation was always supportive of the work of the missionary organisations administered through the Church Missionary Society [CMS]. During the period of his ministry, the Rev. P.J Martin was the church's CMS Chairman and the secretary was Mrs Joyce Smith who wrote a detailed account of the meetings spanning 1945-59. In the early years the committee met in the choir vestry. It was their job to distribute and collect the missionary "boxes" and arrange events designed to educate and raise much-needed funds.

A Missionary Pageant was held in church from 6th -16th May 1945. A more ambitious project was centred at the Parish Room during May 1949. This time they concentrated on an exhibition of the work in India, Pakistan, Africa and the Middle East. A full-sized Bedouin tent was the big attraction. The four-day event included guest speakers, book stalls and teas prepared by the Mothers' Union. The speakers were Canon R.B Jolly, Vicar of St.Mary's; Mr Ralph Tweddle, Headmaster of Sladen Church of England Secondary Modern School; Dr. G.K Beatty and Mr G.L Mallam who was listed as formerly in the Indian Political Service and "*curate designate of this parish* ". Daily tickets cost 1/- or a season ticket at 2/6d.

In 1950 the committee combined with the Ruri-Decanal committee to "Adopt a Leper" under a scheme organised by the British Empire Leprosy Relief Association. Also in 1950, an article in the Daily Telegraph explained that over 1,200 lepers were being treated and that the King and Queen sponsored two children in Nigeria. The cost of treatment was £5 per annum.

Regular donations were given to the British & Foreign Bible Society and the Rwanda Mission boxes were popular, cast in the shape of a mud-hut. In the early 1950s over ninety boxes were in circulation. Leslie Guest attended a course in Hertfordshire and returned with some interesting films that were projected at Missionary Evenings in the parish room. Representatives from St.Andrew's and Hoobrook attended the committee meetings and later, Capt. Wisken, representing the new church hall on the Comberton Estate, joined them.
The recorded minute book ended in 1959 when the Rev. P.J Martin left the parish.

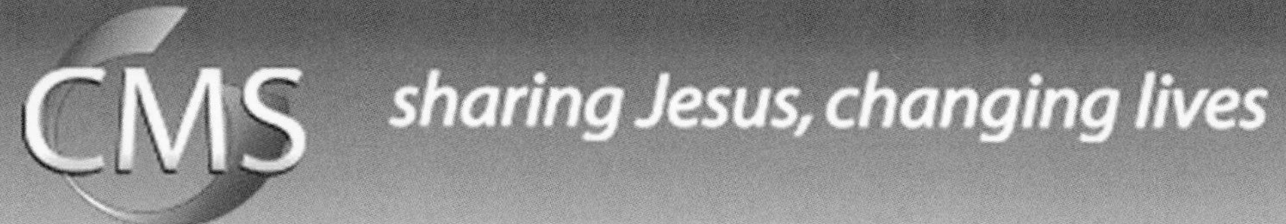

BBC Sunday Half Hour

Although television was increasing in popularity some of the radio programmes were equally popular especially "old faithfuls" such as Desert Island Discs and Sunday Half Hour. The reputation of the church and its choir had reached Broadcasting House and so, on Sunday 13th October 1957, the world tuned in to the BBC Light Programme and the General Overseas Service for thirty minutes of community hymn singing under the title "*Sunday Half Hour from St.George's Church in Kidderminster* ". Richard Maddock, who was the weekly presenter, introduced the hymns. The Producer was the Rev. William Purcell who was responsible for religious broadcasting in the Midlands. In fact the service had been pre-recorded in church on Sunday 6th October. Harold Evers conducted the choir and congregation and Mrs Vera Summers was the organist. Eight well-known hymns were sung including "Rock of Ages" and, once again, "For All the Saints".

The Rev. Leonard Whitehead Chidzey - Vicar 1959-1969

The Rev. Leonard Chidzey in conversation with the Author at a fellow chorister's wedding in 1962

In 1959 the Rev. Leonard W Chidzey became Vicar of St.George's. The former Church Army Captain was a family man with two daughters and, during his ten years in office, did much to improve the fabric of the church. He moved into the Leswell Street Vicarage that had been redecorated and modernised. He wasted no time in getting things moving. Within his first year he had organised a "*Weekend of Prayer and Gifts* " specifically aimed at raising finance to purchase a house in Chester Road South at a cost of £2,270 as a home for the curate. The second part of the appeal needed £1,800 towards a programme of improvements to the Church Hall in Hoobrook. He organised and distributed letters and gift-boxes and on the weekend nearest St.George's Day in April 1960 he sat outside church from 9.00 am till 5.00 pm each day to receive the gifts. The effort was worthwhile and a considerable amount of money was raised.

He became the Rev. Canon Chidzey towards the end of his ministry before taking an appointment in the parish of Driffield in Yorkshire. Many of the congregation kept in touch and Norman Tatlow organised a parish outing to Driffield in October 1975. They were welcomed to tea by the Chidzey family at the Rectory.

Hoobrook School becomes a Church Hall

St.George's continued its ministry to the Hoobrook community with regular Sunday services held in the day school room. Initially they were every two weeks with a Morning Communion alternating with an afternoon Evensong. Cecilia Johnson had also developed a well-attended Sunday School with around 100 scholars and space was becoming a serious problem.

In October 1934 a meeting had been held in the hall adjacent to the Viaduct public house to discuss the future and study some plans for a separate building. At the time the Rev. B.J Isaac was vicar of St.George's.

In the years following further schemes were put forward but little headway was made due to the cost. There was good support and in another ledger headed "*Hoobrook Church Hall 1934-1951*" it is recorded that early benefactors included The Carpet Manufacturing Company, Earl Baldwin of Bewdley, Mr. G.R Woodward, Mrs. Johnson, the Rev. P.J Martin and a good income from the "Mile of Pennies".

During this time it was observed that the number of children attending the day school was significantly declining.

In 1954 the *Sunday Mercury* newspaper featured Hoobrook Infants School in an article charting life in a typical village school.

In the photographs the Headmistress, Olwen Harris, is seen reading poetry from the blackboard and showing the children a playground game.

Two years after the photograph was taken the school closed with the remaining children being transferred to Lea Street School. The school building was subsequently sold to St.George's for a few hundred pounds and plans commenced for its expansion into a larger Church Hall.

It was around this time that Mrs Cecilia Johnson retired from the Sunday School after so many years of dedicated service and she was presented with a bouquet of flowers. She died in August 1951 aged 89 years.

In the photograph she is seated centrally holding the bouquet which had been presented by Derek Woodward [son of Dick Woodward] who is standing behind. Also in the photograph, the Rev. P.J Martin and th three Sunday School teachers who were all members of the Redding family. Shirley, th author's wife, is standing to the right of Derek Woodward.

In 1959 the Parochial Church Council approached the Diocese of Worcester for a loa towards the cost of converting the school to a Church Hall. This application wa supported by the fact that the Hoobrook community was still growing. New counc houses had been built in the late 1930s and there was talk of two blocks of high-ris flats to be built opposite [Thames and Avon House completed in 1970].
The loan was agreed and the figure added to the money donated during the 1960 Gi Day organised by the Rev. L.V Chidzey who had just succeeded Re P.J Martin. The Rev. Chidzey becam a staunch supporter of the projec Local fundraising centred on soci events and whist drives and so th work got under way. A new entranc kitchen and toilets were added an the old outside toilets became a stor In May 1962, with the initi conversion completed, Hoobrook Church Hall was officially opened.

In the following years further developments added a Sanctuary and Vestry with some c the furniture, including the Cross dated 1908, coming from St.Andrew's Missio Church which had closed in 1967. The Altar came from the redundant Swedenborgia Church on Comberton Hill. A folding screen was fitted to hide the Sanctuary when th main room was being used for social events. The new additions were dedicated in Ma 1968. The photograph was taken around that time.

St. Andrew's Mission Church - the final years

The winter of 1947 was the year of the "big freeze", with rationing for most commodities still in place. Coal was in short supply and deliveries intended for St.George's boilers were diverted to Mill Street Hospital. St.Andrew's Church, once again, played its part in parish life with all services being transferred for seven weeks until the freeze ended and coal stocks recovered.

St.Andrew's had its own dedicated congregation which was for many years led by the popular Walter Hill who was Reader-in-Charge. He lived in Offmore Road and died in 1963 aged 83 years. He was buried in St.George's Churchyard.
Another name synonymous with St.Andrew's at the time was their organist and choirmaster Mr R.F Yarrington who led a good robed choir. In later years he was succeeded by Robert [Bob] Ferguson and, even later, Charles Harris.
In the 1950s picture above, taken outside St.Andrew's, Walter Hill can be seen together with Bob Ferguson and the choir.

In 1960 St.Andrew's Church was 70 years old and in need of redecoration and so Humphries & Bowdler Ltd. of Lark Hill gave the walls and gables two coats of paint at a cost of £135. The builder, Councillor Harry Humphries, lived in Chester Road South and was another active member of St.George's Parochial Church Council. In 1957 he was Mayor of Kidderminster.

From the time of its consecration a hand-written minute book entitled "*St.Andrew's Mission Church, Kidderminster 1890* " faithfully recorded the discussions and decisions of the vestry meetings. The first meeting was held on 7th April 1890 with the Rev. T.W Church, the Rev. C.E Newcomb and Rev. E.J Barfeet in attendance together with wardens J Wallis and S Williams.

Walter Hill in St.Andrew's Church

The last entry was dated 7th March 1967 when the Rev. Nigel Fox, curate of St.George's, chaired the meeting.

In May 1962 a letter was received from the Kidderminster Borough Council addressed to St.George's Parochial Church Council. It gave advance notice of their plans for the second phase of the inner ring road and its adverse affect on St.Andrew's Church. The letter talked about compulsory purchase and broached the subject of compensation. However, it was some time later that the plans came to fruition and compensation was agreed.

And so, after 78 years of service to the community St.Andrew's Mission Church closed its doors for the last time following a Civic Service on Sunday 26th November 1967.

The vicar of St.George's, Canon L.W Chidzey, led the service and the Bishop of Worcester preached the last sermon. St.George's choir sang the anthem "O Pray for the Peace of Jerusalem" and the lessons were read by the Mayor, Councillor Harry Purcell, and Lt-Colonel E.R Newcomb who represented the family of the original donor.

The total compensation for St.Andrew's was only £5,000.

Two years later following a fire, St.Andrew's, still affectionately known as the "tin church", was demolished and the land subsequently became part of the Worcester Cross Ringway.

The photograph was taken in 1969 just before demolition.

Christmas and the Nativity

Christmas is always an active time for the family and the church. The annual Sunday School Nativity play dominates the Family Service on the Sunday before Christmas. But the normal congregation probably do not realise that the day schools of the area also come to church for their Nativity production. A lot of hard work goes into the preparation and the children eagerly await the selection of the cast. The costumes provided an ideal opportunity to find a use for those old curtains and blankets!

In the picture, taken in church in 1962, the children of St.George's School pose for their Nativity family photograph. At the time the Headmaster was Arthur Gwillam, another stalwart member of the congregation who served on many of the church committees. His wife, Gwen, was the school secretary and they remained at St.George's School in George Street for twelve years before leaving in 1970. However, times were changing and government finance was now available to modernise the older school buildings - or demolish them!

Church of England Schools

As the education systems for the country developed the churches became less involved, both in administration and the provision of any finance. By the 1970s a number of new "modern" schools were being built in the developing areas of town. The old school buildings were now outdated and were either given another use or replaced.

The first St.George's School to be affected was the Worcester Cross Infants School that had closed in the 1940s and remained empty for the years following. In the late 1960s it was completely demolished as the bulldozers prepared the ground for the new ring road.

In the 1970s a new St.George's Church of England First School was built in Plane Tree Close near Baxter Gardens and it was sad to see the old 150-year-old building in George Street demolished in 1978. The photographs above record the early stages. The photograph below shows the housing development that was subsequently built and the former Parish Room, now called The Fred Bennett Centre, which is still there and in regular use.

Note: In the "Inkwells & School Bells" section of Michael Hale's book he paints an amusing picture of life at St.George's School in its heyday.

For many years a small addition to the school building in Offmore Road housed St.George's Social Club. This building was also part of the demolition programme. Although not officially connected to the church the club was used by some of the congregation who lived in the area. They had an active bowls team that played on the bowling green of St.George's Park and, perhaps, it was this fact that encouraged them to invest in a new building bordering the churchyard in Radford Avenue. The full story is told in Chapter 11 on page 122.

Leswell Street First School, as it was ultimately titled, survived a little longer until a reorganisation closed the school in 1983. Licensed Reader Robin Burford had been a teacher for a number of years and she was the last Headmistress. A service was held in church for the former staff and pupils with a sermon preached by the Rev. P.J Martin. The building remained and was sold to the Probation Services in 1984.

St.Chad's Church Hall

The after-war recovery period of the early 1950s saw the building of a number of new council housing estates around the town. Within the parish was the Comberton Estate which was planned with over 500 new houses. St.George's was allocated one of the houses for its curate. The first occupant was the Rev. G.E Weaver who had the immediate task of setting up a structure of home visits. However, as the houses were occupied and the estate grew it became apparent that a centre for community activities and a place of worship was needed, and the concept of a multi-purpose Church Hall was agreed.

A green-field location on Burcher Green was identified and the plans were drawn. A committee of laymen chaired by Mr E.H.O Carpenter, Chairman of The Carpet Manufacturing Company, was appointed to work with the vicar, the Rev. P.J Martin, and his team to oversee the project.
By this time the Rev. Martin's assistant was Captain R.D Wisken of the Church Army and he became very popular within the local community.

The final building cost was estimated at £8,000 and the figure was achieved with funding from the Bishop of Worcester's Appeal Fund together with some generous local donations. Architect M.W Jones ARIBA was appointed together with builders C&L Walker Ltd.

St.Chad's Church Hall was subsequently built and dedicated at an evening service on Wednesday 23rd May 1956 by the Right Rev. Dr. Mervyn Charles Edwards, Lord Bishop of Worcester.
A Procession of Witness that started at St.George's Leswell Street Vicarage preceded the dedication service.

ST. CHAD'S CHURCH/HALL
COMBERTON
KIDDERMINSTER
(Parish of St. George)

Dedication Service
WEDNESDAY, 23rd MAY, 1956
at 8-0 p.m.

Souvenir Programme

Faculties

For any improvements or alterations to the church or its fabric permission has to be obtained from the Diocese of Worcester. If sanctioned, a legal document called a "faculty" is issued.

While most of the faculties are straight forward requests for additions designed to improve the church, one or two pose a question. For example, in July 1951 a request was granted to fit a bell push in the churchwarden's seat near the main west doors. Presumably a bell would ring somewhere but this was not specified - was it ever installed?

On a more serious note, in 1954 permission was granted for major structural work to the upper part of the tower particularly the apex stones, buttresses, fluorinated caps and the pinnacles. The Midland Electricity Board was called in to replace old wiring and install new electrical lighting and power points. In the same year the brass Processional Cross, donated in memory of Phyllis May Humphries, first came into use.

In 1958 permission was received for the addition of a cycle shed near the choir vestry, the erection of a flagstaff on top of the tower and the levelling of some of the churchyard gravestones. It was reported that two hundred headstones had illegible wording and the necessary statutory notices were posted. However, it was not until ten years later that the stones were removed and the details sent to the Diocesan Registrar. This action effectively restarted burials but, for some, cremation was the answer followed by the burial of the ashes in the graveyard with a small plaque.

These are just a few examples covering the range of faculties that have been issued. It is also a necessity that any unwanted items need a faculty before they can be sold or disposed of - some of these are detailed in earlier chapters.

Note: In the Appendix of this book is a comprehensive list of all plaques, inscriptions and donations. Some of the items required a faculty - others did not.

More about the 1960s

The so-called swinging sixties was a prosperous time for the town as the carpet industry re-carpeted the world in the boom years following the Second World War. This prosperity was reflected in church life as the organisations flourished with good membership.

The September 1961 issue of the Parish Magazine contains reports on the Church of England Men's Society; the Mothers' Union and its independent Young Wives Group; the Women's Guild and the Young People's Fellowship [YPF].

The Sunday School was large and met in the afternoon; the choir stalls were full with a waiting list for the boys' section and St.George's Boy Scouts and Girl Guides, together with the Cubs and Brownies, led a very active life.

Over the years the annual day event known as the "Church Fete" had been held at a number of locations including Aggborough, The Shrubbery and Fairlawn in Comberton. However, by the 1960s the Fete had run its course and had been replaced by the Parish Garden Party generally held in June when the evenings were long.
For many years Mr. & Mrs. Stanley Goodwin allowed their home and gardens at Comberton Hall to be used. The Hall was situated on the corner of Barnett's Lane where it joins Comberton Road - today a housing development. The extensive lawns and gardens against the backdrop of the old hall provided the perfect setting for a social event for the whole parish.

On such occasions the YPF was always in attendance. It had a large membership and an active committee organising social events and outings. Weekly meetings, held in the Parish Room on Tuesday evenings, attracted young people from the whole parish and beyond. Over the years a number of marriages had resulted from these meetings.

Marriage in church was the norm, especially in September when there was an Income Tax advantage to be realised. In the photograph, taken in September 1960, the author is married to his wife, Shirley, whom he met at the YPF. In a service conducted by the Rev. Leonard Chidzey the choir turned out in full and Harold Evers can be seen looking down from the organ loft.

Bert Hinton, who is standing at the nave end on Cantori, sang an alto solo at the groom's request. However, he was not only an accomplished singer, he was also a talented welder and, in June 1961, he made and presented the wrought-iron main gates that are today known as the "angel gates". He also made the Advent candleholder and a number of other wrought-iron flower stands.

More gifts to the church were received with faculties issued for a Litany Desk in memory of Lillian Maud Fawcett who, although blind, taught in the Sunday school for over 50 years. Also, two matching stone flower urns near the chancel steps were donated by the Brown and Summers families.
In 1964 a new altar dorsal curtain with matching pelmet was hung on the east wall. Made by Rackhams of Birmingham the deep red design replaced the original blue and gold curtain that had been in position since the rededication.

At church, the festivals continued to be popular with good congregations but at normal services attendance was decreasing as people found other things to do. The standard of living was improving and, by now, most families had a car. Other attractions, such as television, competed for people's free time and the churches were experiencing a significant decline in attendance and income. Something had to be done.

Christian Stewardship

For many years the church had raised planned finance through a free-will offering scheme with numbered envelopes. For a period it was called the "Duplex Fund" where the giving could be channeled specifically to revenue or capital items. However, the scheme needed a review and, in the early 1960s, "Stewardship" became the buzzword.
Stewardship was a new word with a new meaning for the average parishioner. And so, between February and April 1962, the Diocese of Worcester led a campaign to explain matters and ask people to consider a regular financial gift to the church. A team of consultants called Stewardship Directors Ltd. were engaged and they visited each parish in turn to advise on how to set the wheels in motion. Two parish dinners were organised in the Town Hall and a number of training meetings were held.

A leaflet, containing messages from the Bishop, the vicar and the churchwardens, was sent to each household in the parish explaining the advantages of planned giving and the possible tax advantages. Households in doubt or needing further information were visited by one of the trained volunteers. Initially it was hard going but, as time went by, people's fears diminished and the Stewardship Scheme became a success. In subsequent years renewal campaigns have topped up the income in line with inflation.

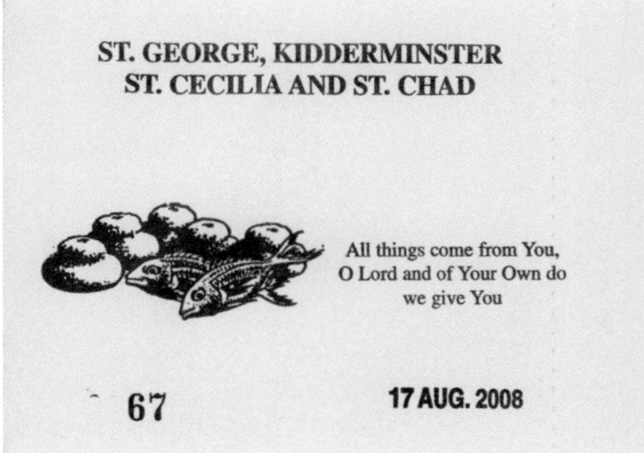

ST. GEORGE, KIDDERMINSTER
ST. CECILIA AND ST. CHAD
All things come from You,
O Lord and of Your Own do
we give You
67
17 AUG. 2008

The 2008 Stewardship envelope

New bells - that play a tune !

Alderman Sir George Eddy OBE JP, former Mayor of Kidderminster, had seen and heard it all. He was the owner of Hepworth's chemical works just down the road from St.George's in Coventry Street. In a newspaper article he made a tongue-in-cheek comment about St.George's bell suggesting that he was "*fed up with the monotonous single dong coming from the tower* " and so he decided to do something about it.

With his eighty-fifth birthday approaching he offered to replace the two existing bells and install a set of bells capable of playing a full chime. It was his way of celebrating his birthday. Discussions took place at John Taylor's Loughborough Foundry and it was

agreed to remove the two existing bells and use the metal to cast six new smaller ones. It will be recalled that the existing bells, installed for the rededication, had been cast from the metal recovered from the original 1824 bells. Sir George and Lady Eddy were present at the foundry as the new bells were cast. Produced in the key of B natural - No.1 is 20 ins diameter and weighs 1.5 cwt; No.2 is 22 ins and 2 cwt; No.3 is 24 ins and 2.75 cwt; No.4 is 26 ins and 3.5 cwt; No.5 is 29 ins and 4.75 cwt and No.6 is 32 ins and 6.3 cwt. [20 cwt equals 1 ton]

The fire of 1922 had affected the structure of the tower and so the new proposal avoided the need to swing the bells by mounting them statically with external hammers striking the outside rim. The hammers were controlled by an electrically operated system supplied by John Smith & Sons of Derby. Local electrician H.M Jefferies of Comberton Hill installed the wiring to a control station in the switch room at ground floor level near the southwest side door. Three peels are available -

1. The "service call" with all six bells playing "rounds".
2. A single tolling unit - installed with Sir George's blessing!
3. A chiming unit playing simple hymn tunes such as "We love the place O God".

The dedication by the Bishop of Worcester, the Right Rev. Mervyn Charles Edwards, took place at Evensong on Sunday 5th May 1963.

In the photograph Sir George Eddy, in his Civic Robes, performs the opening ceremony by unveiling a plaque. Pictured from the left - the Mayor of Kidderminster, Councillor R Oakley; the Rev. L.W Chidzey; Churchwardens Basil Gethin and Stan Buckley and the Bishop of Worcester.

This was the fourth set of bells Sir George had donated to local churches the others being St.John's, St.Barnabas' and St.Mary's.

Faculties and events

The Archdeacon of Dudley came to church on Sunday 22nd September 1963 to dedicate new choir screens. Made by Messrs E.W Perks they were dedicated to a former chorister, George Henry Randall who is pictured with the 1936 choir.

At the same service the first sound amplification system was also dedicated. In this day and age it seems incredible that it was not until the 1960s that normal speech was amplified in such a large volume church with its acknowledged acoustical problem. The system has long since been replaced but it was state-of-art at the time. A large plaque on the south wall details the gift. The wording is reproduced in the Appendix.

In December 1963, on the Sunday before Christmas, BBC Radio again visited St.George's with a Christmas outside broadcast service led by the Rev. Chidzey.

The volume of traffic in Coventry Street was increasing and it became difficult to park by the main gate for weddings and funerals and so, in 1963, the current tree-lined driveway was adopted with hard standing parking for cars.

The Parish Church of APRIL 1970

St. George, *Kidderminster*

with

St. Cecilia, Hoobrook & St. Chad, Comberton

The *Kidderminster Shuttle* published this picture of St.George's Womens' Guild in 1963 when the Rev. Leonard Chidzey and the curate, the Rev. Ken Griggs, attended to receive a cheque for £8 towards the work of the Leprosy Mission.

In 1967 an anonymous donor presented 160 hassocks and a new carpet was fitted in the Sanctuary area as the gift of the Gethin family. The carpet's design featured a Tudor rose on a royal blue background. It was said that Adam Carpets originally wove it for the visit of the Queen to Kidderminster in 1957!

In September 1967 the church celebrated the centenary of the formation of the parish of St.George. This involved a programme of events and services with guest preachers. The first service, on Sunday 24th, saw all the young people of the parish organisations brought together for a special service addressed by the Rev. Wallace Cox, Vicar of St.Mary's. On the same evening the Civic Leaders of the town were invited to a Festival Evensong.

The Town Hall was the venue for a lavish parish party on the following Wednesday. It proved to be a sell-out as tickets were snapped up at 2/6d [25p]. Canon L.W Chidzey made a short address before a small quartet from the choir sang popular songs.

St.George's had always retained a good relationship with the Church Army and, on the following Sunday, Evensong was replaced by an informative series of films presented by Captain W Thompson. The programme continued with a Wednesday "Centenary Festival of Praise" in church and it all ended with the Harvest Festival Services. At the morning Family Service the preacher was the Rev. Leslie Guest who, at the time, was the vicar of Norton near Evesham.

Returning to more mundane issues, the Parochial Church Council became concerned about the mess created by the pigeons that were nesting in the tower. Experts were consulted and suitable netting installed.

Further organ improvements 1968

The Foskett Two Manual Organ, originally installed in 1929, had provided good service but it was not until 1947 that it received a good clean and the addition of some minor improvements. Despite this work there were still problems and another fundraising programme was launched. During 1968, with funds available, the organ was enlarged with a new electro-pneumatic action and other significant additions. Laurence Snell of Tenbury Wells carried out the work after consultation with Harold Evers and his colleague Harold Frampton.

The organ was encased with new oak paneling made by the local joiners Messrs E.W Perks.

Canon Leonard Chidzey dedicated the improvements on 12th October 1968.

In the photograph from the left - Lawrence Snell, Harold Evers and Christopher Robinson who, on the evening of Saturday 2nd November, played at a celebration concert with work by the composers Bach, Sweelinck, Rheinberger, Parry, Mathias and ending with Mozart's Fantasia in F Minor. At the time Christopher Robinson was Organist and Master of the Choristers at Worcester Cathedral. Also in the picture assistant organist Michael Wood can be seen in the organ loft.

A temporary shortage of choirboys around this time prompted Harold Evers to experiment with the introduction of a small group of young ladies to help out. They were never robed and sat on chairs to the side. This was observed and became the subject of a minute at the next Parochial Church Council meeting - more boys were recruited and the problem was solved.

The Rev. Hubert Edward Montague-Youens - Vicar 1969-1972

In January 1969 the Rev. Hubert Edward Montague-Youens became vicar having previously been Vicar of Kempsey near Worcester. He was a family man with a ready smile and a good, and infectious, sense of humour.
During his relatively short stay he introduced a number of changes that the church, and the daughter churches, benefit from today. He was not short of help and had the assistance of two Curates and an active Licensed Reader. His friendship with local artist Muriel Robinson paid dividends as she prepared some excellent visual aids for the family services. Muriel's father was Joseph Benjamin Robinson who was the churchwarden at the time of the rededication.

Since the rededication, the clergy had sat in the reserved positions in the rear choir stalls. The choir was large and seating became a problem, particularly at the festivals. With a donation of two carved oak clergy prayer desks and seats the Rev. Montague-Youens took the opportunity to organise timber extensions to the chancel steps and create two independent positions for the clergy - these positions remain today. It should also be recorded that he introduced the current altar cloth and frontal.

He took a keen interest in the daughter churches and it was under his guidance that early plans for the further development of St.Chad's Church came to fruition.

He left St.George's in 1972 to become Rector of Ribbesford with Bewdley and Dowles more commonly referred to as St.Anne's, Bewdley. Later, in 1976, he was appointed Rural Dean of Kidderminster and two years later made an Honorary Canon of Worcester Cathedral.

Church government

By the "Synodical Government Measures 1969" the Church Assembly renamed and restructured itself under the new title the General Synod of The Church of England. Local changes saw the establishment of three Team Ministries under the leadership of St.Mary's Vicar, the Rev. Ian Griggs. The teams were St.Mary's, St.George's and St.John's. The St.George's Team, led by the Rev. Montague-Youens, reported on the affairs of St.George's Parish including St.Chad's and St.Cecilia's.
The linking of the town's resources paid off when, in 1971, staff shortages at Sladen School saw St.George's Curate, the Rev. Philip Darby a former schoolmaster, assisting for four periods a week.

The halcyon days of the choir

In 1971 the choir was strong with sixteen men and an abundance of boys. In the picture the choir is resplendent in new blue choir cassocks and white surplices. The robes were first worn at the 1969 Nine Lessons and Carols service and they replaced the much-darned and shabby black cassocks that dated back to 1927.
For the boys white ruffles now replaced the Eton collars and bow ties.
The photograph shows the assembled choir and clergy seated on the chancel steps.
In the front row from the left - Major Bill Perks, Warden; Basil Gethin, Church Warden Emeritus; the Rev. Philip Darby, Senior Curate; Harold Evers; the Rev. Edward Montague-Youens; the Rev. David Bird, Curate; Jack Mowate, Licensed Reader; Norman Tatlow, Choir Secretary and Fred Knowles, Warden.
In the back row, extreme left a young Tim Morris standing next to Bert Hinton, also seventh from the left is Fred Buckley who had been a choirboy at the rededication service. The author stands at the extreme right of the back row. Also standing, left John Gwillam; Bob Scott; Michael Wood and extreme right Harold Pritchard.
From the current choir [2008] a young Ross Webb stands behind Harold Evers and Adrian Sewell behind Bill Perks to the left just in front of Peter Tatlow, Norman's son.

In the days before voice amplification Bill Perks was an asset because he had been a Major in the Royal Engineers and when he spoke in church his "parade square" diction and volume left no one in any doubt as to what was said. He was Works Manager at Adam Carpets and a director of the Kidderminster Building Society. He was also a very influential member of the Parochial Church Council.

Membership of the choir was like being in a club. Many of the senior members had a long service and some of the boys had graduated to the back row when their voice broke.
The social calendar was extensive. The annual choirboy's party and the full-day choir outing were the highlights. For many years a choir dinner for the senior choristers and invited guests gave an opportunity for St.George's Male Voice Quartet to perform. Formed in the 1940s it consisted of Bert Hinton alto, tenor Harold Pritchard, baritone Bob Scott and Harold Evers who sang bass and played the piano. They sang a variety of songs and ballads, "Linden Lea" being a favourite. In later years Norman Tatlow took the bass line.

"*When I was a choirboy* " was an article written by the author for the Parish Magazine some years ago. It has been reproduced in "Hassocks and Cassocks" and conveys the more humorous side of life in the choir. However, one story that has not been told concerns the Rev. Edward Montague-Youens and a certain choirboy who constantly chattered during the sermons. It eventually became too much for the vicar who paused and with a smile on his face named the boy and pronounced, "... *do you mind shutting up while I am trying to preach my sermon!* " much to the amusement of the congregation and choir.

A little more

Soon after the photograph was taken Mary Morris [Tim's Grandmother] donated a grand piano to the church in memory of her husband, Henry Arthur Morris. The piano, made by Schiedmayer of Stuttgart, proved a great asset at choir practices and replaced a very old harmonium that had seen good service for many years previous [probably the American Organ referred to earlier]. Following a faculty the harmonium was sold for £5 in 1973.

There was always a need to raise money and in 1970 the Rev. Montague-Youens combined the April Patronal celebrations with a Festival of Flowers and Crafts. The three-day festival started on the Friday and on all days a "*Silver collection in aid of parochial funds* " was requested. In church, twenty-nine individual exhibits were on display prepared by the flower clubs of Franche, Broadwaters, Worcester, Hagley, Stourport, Wilden and Halesowen. Individual displays used the theme of the Spinning Wheel, a Maypole, the Potter's Wheel and the Blacksmith.

Traditionally the Altar had been positioned directly against the east wall with the celebration of Holy Communion taken from the front. Although the date is not recorded it was during the 1960s that the Altar Table was moved forward thus providing access to the rear for the clergy to administer communion.

At the start of the 1970s an air of optimism prevailed. However, there were more changes around the corner and the church was to lose some old friends.

Chapter 11 Changing times - 1970s and into the 80s

The 1970s was a time of change. The carpet industry was still thriving despite the after-war boom coming to an end. The town took on a different look as the third and final stage of the ring road was opened to traffic in 1973. A new shopping mall called the Swan Centre with its integral multi-storey car park was the place to shop. Crown House dominated the Bull Ring and, nearby, another multi-storey car park built in Pitts Lane on the site of a former spinning mill.

While the church and the churchyard had not changed its appearance over the years the surrounding area had sustained significant development. A new housing estate now occupied the land bordering the northern and eastern perimeters of the churchyard. From Radford Avenue a new road, christened Gilbert Scott Way, led into the estate with Harold Evers Way branching from it.
St.George's Social Club was the new building on the corner near the Gilbert Scott intersection.

St. George's Social Club

While the church had started the Social Club in the 1930s it no longer retained any direct links other than in the name. However, the club has an interesting history and Stuart Manser has prepared the following based on information in his keeping -

" The club adjacent to the church in Radford Avenue originated and grew from its close association with St.George's Church. St.George's Young Men's Club was established in 1921 with the Parochial Church Council's [PCC] financial support and they met in the Parish Room in George Street. A review of church affiliated accommodation in 1930 identified the potential of using rooms at the rear of the near-by St.George's Junior School.

St.George's Old Boy's Association, known locally as the Social Club, was already meeting in the building but they had a declining membership and they arranged a meeting with the vicar, the Rev. B.J Isaac, and the PCC. The meeting resulted in a letter to the PCC in 1932 officially handing over the Association's affairs to the church. At 7 pm on Monday 30th October 1932 the St.George's Men's Club was opened by Mr. H Silk, the first President. It was available to "*all young men over 17 years of age, who either lived in the Parish, or worshipped at the Parish Church or St.Andrew's* ".
Here the roots of the present day club were established.

The entrance to the building was in Offmore Road. There was a main room 25 feet square and a smaller room 25 feet by 13 feet. By November 1935 the Club was 60 strong and, following a request from its members, a Young Men's Bible Class was established on Sunday afternoons. However, the main social activity was bagatelle and billiards.
The PCC continued to look after and maintain the premises but a request by club members for a "sale of liquor" licence was not well received. It took three years for the PCC to relent and finally agree to the licence in July 1938.

When the Rev. B.J Isaacs took up his wartime chaplaincy duties the Rev. P.J Martin became actively involved in overseeing the club's affairs in his dual role as incumbent of the church and chairman of the club. During the war years, with men away on active service, wives of members were, for the first time, allowed to join. While the club was successful in local competitions of bagatelle, billiards and darts, the piano was the main form of in-house social entertainment.

Membership increased again after the Second World War with a limit set at 130. Bowling, fishing and cards were added to the list of activities. The Rev. Martin was made a Vice President and the club retained a representative on the PCC. In return the church had two representatives on the club's committee. Financial support for the church came from individual members and the club's donations to the Gift Days and Garden Fetes.

The club continued to thrive in membership and became financially independent of the church for repairs and maintenance. They built a new toilet block in 1951. In 1953 Mr. C Bint was the club's representative on the PCC and he became the their first Life Member.

In February 1954 it changed its name to Saint George's Social Club.

The Rev. P.J Martin continued to take an interest and remained a Vice President until he left the Parish in 1959. However, in the following years the link with the church diminished ".

In the late 1960s it became apparent that St.George's Junior School was in a state of disrepair and a new school was planned. This was an opportunity for the Social Club to look for new premises and they identified land in Radford Avenue near the church's north perimeter wall. Planning permission was granted in 1968 but it was not until June 1974 that the club opened on its present site.
The location was ideal for the bowling green in the park opposite. The facilities included a bar and social rooms for cribbage and snooker.

Today, the club is still popular and the building now has wider uses with the main rooms available for hire.

The Rev. Peter David Chippendale BA
Vicar 1973-1977

It was also a time of change at St.George's Vicarage as the Rev. Peter Chippendale became vicar in January 1973. He was a family man with a son and two daughters and he came from a more rural part of Worcestershire having been Vicar of Eckington, Defford and Besford near Pershore.

During his ministry he became involved with the Urban Ministry Project that examined the social conditions of our towns and cities. He was also very interested in youth development and many of the older Scouts and Guides of the town will remember his St.George's Day Parade services when he used extraordinary visual aids to put over the point. In his first year he used the "Wombles" theme music in a talk about litter. The second year he brought a fully rigged sailing boat into the chancel. In the following year the local Air Training Corps provided part of an aeroplane. However, the year before he left the parish he pulled off a coup with the driving of an Austin Mini up ramps and into the chancel !

In these years it was the custom to leave the altar cross and candlesticks in position at all times. However, in 1975 they were stolen and something had to be done. And so the vicar, who was an accomplished carpenter, produced his own wooden "Chippendale" cross as a temporary substitute until a new donation was received. Today, it remains in position during the week leaving the proper brass cross and candlesticks safely locked away until the Sunday services.

The Rev. Peter Chippendale left the parish in November 1977 to become Vicar of Holy Trinity, The Lickey.

ST. GEORGE'S FESTIVAL

1824 - 1925 - 1975

7th - 14th September 1975

St. George's Church
Birmingham Road
Kidderminster

50 years celebration - St. George's Festival

In 1975 the church reached another landmark as it celebrated the completion of 50 years since the rededication in 1925. And so, the vicar organised a full week of services and events. An exhibition was set up in church for the week with materials from local industry to add emphasis to the links between the town's industry and St.George's Church.

The week of celebration started on Sunday 7th September with an Opening Festival Service when the Bishop of Dudley, the Right Rev. Michael Mann, was the guest preacher.

During the week the Parish Room was the location for a talk about "Old Kidderminster"; Arthur Wills, Organist of Ely Cathedral, gave a recital in church and, on the following evening, a well-attended Buffet Supper packed the Long Room at Kidderminster Cricket Club. The choirs of the Deanery filled the church on the following Saturday as Roger Judd, Master of Music at St.Michael's College in Tenbury, conducted a choral service with the theme "The Journey".
The Festival ended on the following Sunday when two Bishops were welcomed to the pulpit. The Right Rev. Robin Woods preached at the morning Family Communion and, at Evensong, the popular former Bishop the Right Rev. Mervyn Charles Edwards made a welcome return.

Within a year of the Church's 50th Celebration the vicar, the Rev. Peter Chippendale, was involved with another half century but this time it involved his Organist and Choirmaster Harold Evers.

Harold Evers appointed Borough Organist

Harold Evers retired from paid employment in 1962 when he severed his links with British Steel. He had worked at the former Richard Thomas & Baldwin factory in Wilden for more than 50 years rising to the position of Office Manager. In retirement he had time to pursue his love of music and sport. He became honorary secretary of Kidderminster Cricket Club.

It is not generally known that in 1966 he was offered the position of Organist and Choirmaster at the Parish Church but he declined wishing to remain loyal to St.George's. However, he did accept the position of Borough Organist in succession to his colleague Harold Frampton. One of the highlights of his musical career was to be selected to conduct the Town Hall's Centenary Gala Concert in 1955 when a 50-strong orchestra accompanied a mass choir of over 150 voices as they sang music from Merry England and Handel's Messiah.

The 1977 photograph on the previous page shows the choir, clergy and churchwardens. It was taken against the background of the church porch and shows the Rev. Peter Chippendale flanked by Harold Evers and Tim Morris.
To the left of Harold Evers - the Rev. Jack Mowate, Norman Tatlow and warden Major Bill Perks. Harold Simmonds, also churchwarden, is seated next to Tim Morris. In the first row the gentlemen behind the boys is Ross Webb, the author, John Gwillam, John Geary, Adrian Sewell, Crucifer Fred Buckley, Harold Pritchard and Bernard [Barney] Everard. In the back row, to the left of the cross Peter Tatlow, Mike Pugh, Cliff Taylor and Arthur Rivers who was a former member of St.Andrew's Choir.
Over the years it has been a fact that the children of the gentlemen choristers have formed part of the boys' choir. In this photograph seven of the boys have fathers standing behind them, namely the sons of Messrs Geary with three and Taylor and the author who have two each. Harold Simmonds lived near the vicarage in Leswell Street. His father, Charles, was a quietly spoken gentleman known for his poetry. For many years he had been the Vicar's Warden.

Harold Evers retires in 1976 after 50 years

In 1976 Harold Evers retired after completing 50 years as Organist and Choirmaster at St.George's. He was immediately appointed Organist Emeritus. He personally selected the music for his final Festival Evensong on Sunday 27th June choosing music by Stanford, Wesley's anthem "Blessed be the God and Father" and, at the conclusion, a four-fold Amen of his own composition.
On the scheme of music for the June services he wrote - "*It is with sadness in my heart that I now reluctantly relinquish the high office I have held with considerable pride for the past 50 years, and I wish to offer my everlasting gratitude to the gentlemen and boys of the Choir, and the Assistant Organist, for the magnificent loyalty and service you have so freely given. May God be with you and bless you all* ".
On the following Tuesday he was given a formal presentation in the Town Hall. As an accomplished bass he made occasional "guest" appearances in the choir until his death in 1980. He was cremated and his ashes remain near the church he served so loyally.
[**HE** on the Graveyard plan Chapter 3 page 39].

A new Organist and Choirmaster

For many years the parish magazine carried reports from all the organisations. Harold Evers was the editor and a regular contributor charting life in the choir stalls. The organ restoration fund was always open for contributions and Harold had positioned a large redundant organ pipe for any such donations.

In one of the 1960s magazines he wrote the following - "*I do want to thank my little friend Master Tim Morris for a donation of 10/-. He is most anxious to see our organ completed and I hope his wish will one day be realised* ".
It proved to be a good investment for both parties because Tim, as a very young man, became a member of the choir and assistant organist before eventually succeeding Harold Evers.

Andrew Timothy [Tim] Morris

By profession Tim Morris followed in his father's footsteps becoming a partner in the local estate agent and auctioneer company Phipps & Pritchard who, at the time, had offices in Bank Buildings in the town centre. He later formed his own practice Tim Morris & Associates. He married Jane, Norman Tatlow's daughter, and they have two daughters.

Tim was appointed a Justice of the Peace in 1984 and maintains an organising role with the Royal School of Church Music of which he is the current Area Secretary.
He succeeded Harold Evers in two other appointments. Firstly, as Organist of Kidderminster Town Hall, where he is now the longest serving holder of the post and Chairman of the Hill Organ Promotion Society, and secondly, as Provincial Grand Organist.
He inherited a strong all male choir and vowed to maintain the high standards set by his predecessor. Tim Morris played his first service on Sunday 4th July 1976.
In 1993 he became the church's Director of Music.
In more recent years he has become involved with the local radio station BBC Hereford & Worcester. Particularly their early Sunday morning religious programmes.

The Rev. John Robert Ilson BSc BD - Priest in Charge & Rector 1977-1985

The Rev. John R Ilson came to St.George's as Priest in Charge in 1977. He had previously been Rector of Hooton Roberts with Ravenfield in the Diocese of Sheffield and also Director of Church Schools. In 1981 he was appointed Rector of the St.George's Team Ministry.
A family man with a young son, he remained for the next nine years during which time there was a considerable addition to the church's building.

In 1985 he left St.George's and moved to St.Peter's in the parish of Powick with Callow End where he was Priest in Charge for eleven years. He retired from parochial ministry to become, for the next eight years, Chaplain at the North Devon District Hospital in Barnstaple.

The Church Annexe

The Parish Room had had its day and seemed remote for church life. For a while it was thought to have been part of the compulsory purchase order associated with St.George's School. However, this was not the case but it prompted the Parochial Church Council to examine a number of other alternative locations. These included a new building in Radford Avenue on the site now occupied by the Social Club and a building in the northwest corner of the churchyard where many of the gravestones were old and unattended. In 1980 a third alternative was tabled that seemed to have all the answers. It involved the building of an annexe to the church containing all the amenities that the church lacked.

The Parochial Church Council were enthusiastic and the Rev. John Ilson led the team as proposals were prepared for the clearing of an area, near the church, on the north side of the churchyard for the building of a single storey multi-purpose room with good storage, kitchen and ample toilet facilities.
The proposal connected the annexe to the church via a short covered walkway to the north wall side door.

A faculty was granted and the statutory notices posted regarding the few graves that existed in the chosen area. With no objections to hand, architect H.W Rolley RIBA was engaged to prepare the drawings and local builders George Law successfully bid for the construction work.

The service of dedication took place on Friday 17th July 1981 and was led by the Right Rev. Robin Woods, Lord Bishop of Worcester. Major Bill Perks, Vice Chairman of the Parochial Church Council read one of the lessons and the choir sang the aptly named anthem "Behold, the tabernacle of God".

The Venerable Christopher Campling, Archdeacon of Dudley, performed the actual opening ceremony in the porch of the annexe with the words relayed by the church's amplification system and shown on closed circuit television.

In the photograph, taken at the unveiling of the plaque, from the left A.E [Bert] Carter, Warden; Peter Tatlow, cross-bearer; the Bishop; the Archdeacon and the Rev. John Ilson. Out of picture Norman Tatlow, Warden.

The old Parish Room was subsequently sold and is now known as the Fred Bennett Centre. Photographs on page 55.

The provision of proper and secure toilet facilities rendered the existing outside toilet arrangement redundant and it was demolished. The location can still be seen.

The early 1980s - a busy period

For a number of years the Town Hall was the venue for a short series of concerts by the City of Birmingham Symphony Orchestra. However, the Town Hall was in urgent need of repair and redecoration and they looked for another venue large enough to house the orchestra and seat the large supporting audiences. And so, with the front row of the choir stalls removed and some temporary staging in position St.George's was the ideal venue with members of the congregation acting as ticket sales, ushers and providing the all-important refreshments. There were two series, in 1979 and 1980, before the CBSO returned to the Town Hall.

St.George's Ladies' Fellowship was formed in 1982 and at the same time a Men's Society, both held their monthly meetings in the new annexe facility.

In May 1982 Heatrend Ltd. installed a new heating boiler and system. The gas-fired boiler was located in the old boiler-house with the flue projecting through the flat roof. In church, some of the old 1925 radiators were retained and new ones added.

An inspection of the tower saw steeplejacks Alcock & Wood removing some of the dangerous loose stonework and pinnacles. The smaller stones were laid out in church and offered for sale.

In 1983 a serious water leak in the roof in the northeast corner had caused damage to parts of the organ. Remedial work and a slight rearrangement of the soundboards was entrusted to John Bleney, organ builder of Worcester. At the same time a new oak panelled display was added to face down the north aisle. The latter was dedicated to the memory of Gerald Morris, Tim's father. The Rev. Edward Montague-Youens made a welcome return to dedicate the work in November 1985.

In 1983 the structure of the church committees changed with the formation of a team ministry led by the Team Rector assisted by the Team Vicar. Two parish wardens were also appointed of which one had to be from St.George's. The fundamental change centred on the election of three District Church Councils [DCCs] to independently look after the affairs of St.George's, St.Chad's and St.Cecilia's. A single and separate Parochial Church Council [PCC] was elected to look after the parish as a whole. The first St.George's DCC meeting, under the chairmanship of the Rev. John Ilson, was held on the 20th June 1983 and one of the first decisions was to revise the starting time of the Sunday morning service from 10.00 am to 10.15 am. Two years later the Parish Office was set up at the Rectory requiring a part-time secretary.

One of the BBC's most popular television programmes is the long running "Songs of Praise". In the 1980s the BBC chose to take the outside broadcast unit to the industrial towns around the country and Kidderminster, with its carpet industry, was chosen.

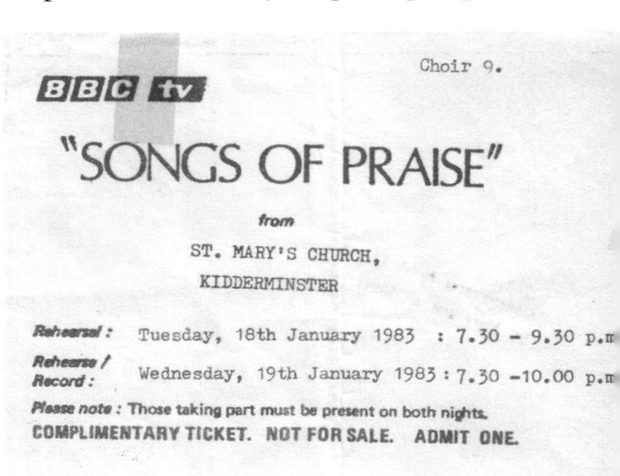
Choir 9.

BBC tv

"SONGS OF PRAISE"

from

ST. MARY'S CHURCH,
KIDDERMINSTER

Rehearsal: Tuesday, 18th January 1983 : 7.30 - 9.30 p.m

Rehearse / Record: Wednesday, 19th January 1983 : 7.30 -10.00 p.m

Please note: Those taking part must be present on both nights.

COMPLIMENTARY TICKET. NOT FOR SALE. ADMIT ONE.

On Wednesday 19th January 1983 the church congregations of the town gathered in St.Mary's to record the programme under the direction of Michael Shoesmith. The church was full to capacity as Tim Morris conducted the hymn singing accompanied by Angela Cattanach-Chell who was the organist at St.Mary's. The programme was introduced by Geoffrey Wheeler.

Charles Wesley's "Ye servants of God", sung to the German tune "Paderborn", was the opening hymn and it raised the roof as the last verse was sung with a rousing descant. The children played their part with the hymn "I am the bread of life".

The Rev. Bill Hopley was the local Industrial Chaplain and he recorded an interview in one of Brinton's town centre weaving sheds. Also interviewed was Lyn Koker and Bob Hale from St.George's parish. The service closed with a blessing by the Rev. Canon Ian Griggs before the closing hymn "All creatures of our God and King".

The full service was broadcast on Sunday 30th January 1983.

In July 1984 BBC Radio returned, this time to St.George's for another Sunday Half Hour conducted by Tim Morris. Again it was a good selection of well-known hymns including William Walsham How's "It is a thing most wonderful". The service ended in grand style with no acoustic problems as the upper voices sang the descant to "Ye Holy Angels bright".

Billy Graham's "Mission England" made a big impact on the spiritual lives of many people. Some of the congregation joined the other town churches as a number of coaches made their way to Villa Park football ground for his midland crusade service.

Musically, St.George's choir retained its reputation and was in demand in other locations. In 1984 they shared the Town Hall stage with the Harry Cheshire School Band in a Family Christmas Carol Concert organised by the Lions. For a number of years following it became a regular event.

Over the years the choir had been invited to sing Saturday Evensong at a number of prestigious locations principally Worcester Cathedral and Pershore Abbey. But in August 1985 they made the long trip to Guildford's modern Cathedral.
In subsequent years the DCC became concerned about the passage of pedestrians through the churchyard to the housing on the east side. This was associated with an increase in vandalism, not only to the church structure but also, in 1985, considerable damage to the gravestones. Notices were posted reminding people that it was not a right-of-way but they had little effect.

"Faith in the City" was the title of a 1985 report authorised by the Arch Bishop of Canterbury's Commission that reported on Urban Priority Areas. In earlier years the Rev. Peter Chippendale had been part of the research team.
The spoken word was also under review with another controversial issue as the Alternative Service Book [ASB] replaced the Book of Common Prayer during 1985.

St. Chad's Church, Burcher Green, Comberton

During the 1960s the congregation continued to grow and there was talk of expansion. In the late 1960s the plans became more detailed as architect James Snell prepared drawings for a new worship area added to the east side of the existing hall and a new entrance on the north side. Inside the church, sliding doors were proposed to separate the two areas giving the option of a larger room for the better-attended services. The cost was estimated at £10,000. Funding became available with help from the "Church Commissioners Grants for New Housing Areas" and so the orders were placed and the work was put in hand.
The act of dedication was performed on 10th October 1971 by the Bishop of Worcester, the Right Rev. Robin Woods at a service led by the then vicar of St.George's, the Rev. Edward Montague-Youens who had done so much to plan and lead the project.

St.Chad's continued to be a growing church community and in 1985 yet another extension was added along the south wall. This addition was dedicated by the Right Rev. Philip Goodrich, Bishop of Worcester on the 21st. September 1985.
Central Television's Pentecost Morning Worship was broadcast from St.Chad's Church on Sunday 22nd May 1988 with the Rev. Michael Mitton leading the worship.

Note : A more detailed account of life at St.Chad's can be found in a booklet put together by Mattie Underhill in May 2006. "St.Chad's Church - 50 Years on Comberton" is a wealth of information with some excellent photographs but, perhaps more importantly, it talks about some of the clergy and the people who have played a part in the life of the daughter church.

Chapter 12 The Barker Years

The Rev. Nicholas John Willoughby Barker BA. MA. - Team Rector 1986 - 2007

In 1986 the Rev. N.J.W Barker came to St.George's as Team Rector. He had qualified at Oriel College, Oxford and Trinity College, Bristol before a curacy in Watford and Team Vicar at Didsbury St.James and Emanuel in Manchester.

"Nick", as he was happy to be known, came with his wife Katherine and their two sons. The Barker family soon settled into the Leswell Street Vicarage, now known as the Rectory, and quickly became part of parish life.
A daughter and another son were added during the next twenty-one years, as he became the second longest serving incumbent. He was appointed Rural Dean of Kidderminster in 2001 and two years later made an Honorary Canon of Worcester Cathedral.

During his long reign as Rector, the church and the parish continued to flourish but there were a number of significant changes in the pipeline. For example, following written authority from the Bishop of Worcester in 1987, he had the job of training selected members of the congregation to administer Communion. Three years later the Church of England had reached a conclusion on the ordination of women to the priesthood and St.George's received its first female curate.

He recalled that it was a wet and windy day when he came for his interview and water was pouring in through the Lady Chapel roof. This prepared him for what was to be his greatest challenge. The main church building, both inside and out, was in need of major and costly repair and it became his job to lead the team in the planning of the work and the raising of the necessary finance.

The church building has problems

An inspection of the church buildings and the surrounding churchyard in 1985 indicated that there were a number of serious issues that needed attention. A report was prepared by the Hagley architect David Mills RIBA and he soon got to know the new incumbent as they sat down to list and cost a phased programme of work.

For many years, in exceptionally bad weather, the main roof had leaked in a number of places and there were problems that needed urgent attention.
In 1987 William Jackson Ltd. of Langley Green was contracted to do the work that involved repairs to the valley gutters on the north and south sides. Also, repairs to the wall plates and the rafter bases that now needed to be reformed and strengthened with new steel bars. New rainwater gullies were also formed at the higher level.

Inside the church, the ingress of water had damaged the plasterwork and a large area of the south wall needed re-plastering and painting. A section of the south aisle floor timbers had also suffered from wet rot and was replaced.

At the rear of the church on the east side the flat roof of the clergy vestry was the subject of dry rot and was subsequently totally removed and replaced. In the tidy-up members of the congregation pulled together as the clergy and choir vestries were cleaned and repainted. Derek Woodward provided new Brintons carpet for the clergy vestry and Mrs Haywood carpeted the choir vestry.
In church the timberwork of the chancel seating was cleaned together with the altar communion rails where a hinged centre section was added.
Other work included the resurfacing of the main approach driveway in 1989. The trees lining the driveway needed pollarding and to keep the churchyard clean "wheelie bins" were positioned near the Radford Avenue entrance. The rector also introduced a Saturday "work day" where volunteers from the congregation gave the church and the churchyard a thorough "spring clean".

The Peace Window

Since the rededication, the prominent east wall Rose Window, with its plain leaded glass, had often been the subject of adverse comment. Colour was needed and in 1987 Miss May Parker provided the funding to convert the window to stained glass, much to the delight of a congregation who played a part in selecting the final design.

Manufactured and installed by Clive Sinclair of the Norgrove Studios in Redditch the window was lined internally with stained glass and protected externally with a polycarbonate sheet. Christened "The Peace Window" it was dedicated by the Bishop of Worcester during Evensong on Sunday 5th June 1988. On the rear outside cover there is a colour photograph - look for the "dove of peace" in the lower radius.

The Rev. Andrea [Andi] Margaret Jones
Curate & Acting Team Vicar 1990 - 1995

In 1990 the General Synod of the Church of England approved the ordination of women to the priesthood and, following her ordination as Deacon in Worcester Cathedral in July 1990, the Rev. Andi Jones was appointed Curate at St.George's. She was ordained to the priesthood in Worcester Cathedral in May 1994 thus becoming one of the first women to be ordained in the Diocese.
In September of that year she became Acting Team Vicar in St.George's Parish.

Andi quickly became popular especially at the daughter churches. After five years' ministry in the parish, in September 1995, she left to work in the Diocese of Lichfield, firstly at St.Aiden, Penn Fields and later St.Andrew at Great Wyrley.

When she retired in 2006 she returned to live in Kidderminster to worship and help out at St.George's.

Church Life

While it was the established practice to hold "Mayor's Sunday" at the Parish Church the tradition was broken on Sunday 21st. June 1987 when the Mayor, Councillor Bronwen Ingham, chose St.George's for her Civic Service.
The Mayor and the Town Clerk, Charles Talbot, read the lessons before the Rev. Nick Barker preached the sermon.

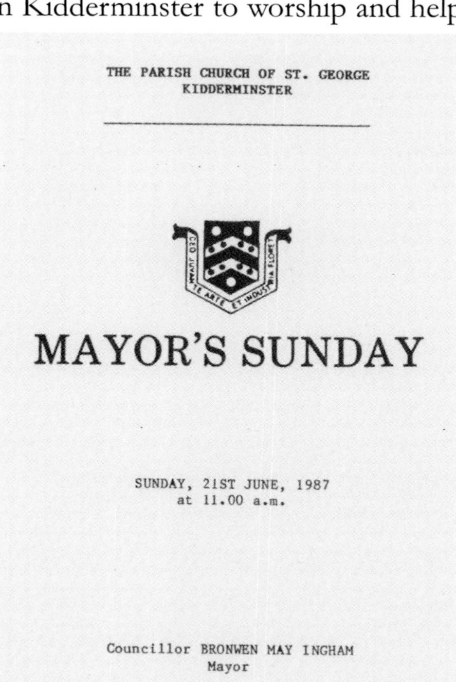

THE PARISH CHURCH OF ST. GEORGE
KIDDERMINSTER

MAYOR'S SUNDAY

SUNDAY, 21ST JUNE, 1987
at 11.00 a.m.

Councillor BRONWEN MAY INGHAM
Mayor

The combined churches ministered to the industry of the area through an Industrial Chaplain who was generally attached to St.Mary's parish team. It was their job to visit the factories and deal with any spiritual matters arising at the workplace.

Some of the Chaplains became well known in the area particularly the Rev. Roger Howes, who was the first appointment, and the Rev. Bill Hopley who featured in the Songs of Praise service reported earlier. In October 1988, St.George's was the home for a weeklong exhibition of the town's industry that culminated in a United Industrial Service in church.

During 1990 the combined churches, under the title Kidderminster United Christian Council [KUCC], held their "Celebration 90" with the Rev. Canon David MacInnes and 120 students coming from St.Aldate's Church in Oxford for a week of events. It was from that time that prayers for healing began at selected morning services.

Restoration Fund and Sponsorship

With such a large church to maintain and the threat of yet more urgent repairs, St.George's Church Restoration Fund, set up around 1990, was always open for donations.

Church income came from a variety of sources including gift days; donations from individuals; the profit from bazaars and craft fairs and loans from the Diocese of Worcester Board of Finance who, from their Worcester Deansway office, were always very supportive of the need to preserve such an important building. The Leswell Trust, set up following the sale of Leswell Street School, was also available for loans. However, there were other ways of helping the cause. For a time members of the congregation took their newspapers to church for recycling; the "Crafters" met on a regular basis and recycled Christmas cards and made needlework items; used stamps, coins and postcards were sorted and sold and Tim Morris organised a Grand Auction with 250 donated lots.

Individuals entered events and took sponsorship. The Rector joined the author in the running of the Wyre Forest Half Marathon and they raised £400. In later years the author also ran the London and New York Marathons for sponsorship split between the Church of England Children's Society and the organ and choir robes funds.

In 1993 the choir and their supporters completed a sponsored walk - walking the length of the Malvern Hills!

Church Life continued

In 1991 both the PCC and the DCC discussed the spiritual state of the church and the parish in a diocese led project entitled "Mission MOT". A ten-point list for consideration included mission, worship, pastoral responsibility, prayer, fellowship, youth, buildings, training, leadership and personal responsibility. Members of the congregation completed a questionnaire.

Mission work abroad had always been on the agenda and the church, in recent years, had developed a special relationship with Sharing of Ministries Abroad [SOMA] and particularly their work in Tanzania.

Crosslinks was another associated organisation with John and Phyll Chesworth forming the contact.

In 1993 the Rector, the Rev. Andi Jones and parishioner Glenn Scott visited them with the Rev. Don Brewin of SOMA. The main objective was to lead a conference in the Kagera Diocese which lies between Lake Victoria and Burundi. They also preached at St.Mary Magdalene's in Kigamboni in Dar es Salaam where they were welcomed by the Rev. Canon Lawrence Mnubi, Priest in Charge. The Rev. Andi Jones commented that, because they did not have women priests in Africa, she was somewhat of a novelty and was treated as an "*honorary man*" during the visit!

Meanwhile, yet another Stewardship Renewal Campaign was launched in 1993 under the title "Giving to God". It had been over thirty years since the scheme had been introduced. One of those responsible for setting it up was Norman Tatlow.

Norman Tatlow

Norman Tatlow was a schoolteacher who came to the parish with his wife Sylvia in 1954. As a talented bass he was soon recruited into Harold Evers' choir. He later took on the job as choir secretary and his enthusiasm and organisational flair produced many daylong choir outings, parties and other events. In 2005 he completed his fifty years as a chorister.

His dedication to the church in general is exceptional. Over the years he has held continuous service with the church councils and for many years acted in the capacity of Church Warden. When he retired from the position in 1987 he was appointed Church Warden Emeritus. "Songs of Praise" may have been a national institution on television but St.George's has its own version in an annual service led by Norman as he introduced hymns chosen by the congregation.

For many years "Tatlow's Tours" provided a well-organised parish day out to some exotic locations including Hampton Court and Buckingham Palace. However, his greatest feat of organisation came in 1980 when he booked a fourteen-day coach tour to the Austrian town of Stams with an excursion to the Oberammergau Passion play.

A new look choir

In 1994 the choir looked resplendent in their new purple choir robes. However, the traditionally all male choir was having difficulties in recruiting boys. In the past replacements had come from the school choirs, particularly Sladen, together with some from the congregation and the sons of the back-row choristers. There seemed to be no solution and so, in 1994, a small "robed" girls choir was formed and trained by Mary Wyatt. Tim Morris's daughters were among the founder members.

In the shops CDs were the latest thing and, in 1998, the choir made its own with the recording of a Advent CD entitled "Lo he Comes" featuring all the popular carols.

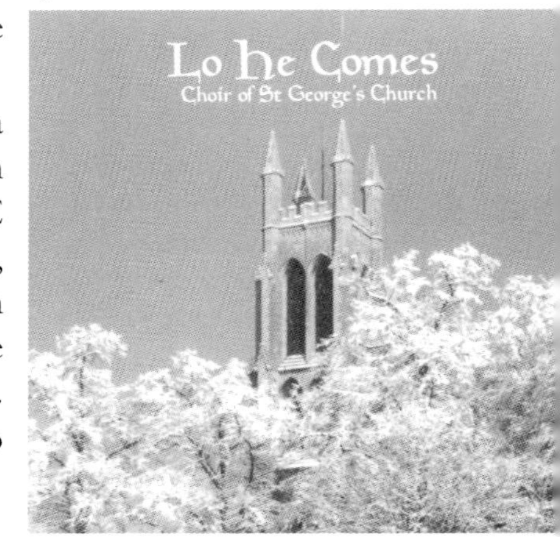

Tim Morris' link with local radio attracted a number of special broadcast services from St.George's including the first recorded BBC Hereford & Worcester Celebration of Christmas, broadcast on the morning of Christmas Day in 1993. "New Beginnings" was the title of the Sunday Service recorded on 13th September 1999. In the years following the church continued to play its part in local religious broadcasting.

St. Cecilia's Church, Hoo Road, Hoobrook

The Hoobrook area house-building programme continued with a new private estate off Hoo Road and so it was decided to make major alterations and extend the building to create a proper church worship area. In September 1985, with the support of a growing congregation, the project was launched with a major fund raising programme. A more practical gift was a "Portacabin" for use by the Sunday School.

It was a major addition to the building with a cost for the initial work estimated at £160,000. By this time the Rev. Nick Barker had replaced the Rev. John Ilson who started the project and he led the team with architect David Mills drafting the proposals for a first phase. A new building was planned with new service mains together with the foundation work for a second phase. Funds became available from individual donations, personal loans, gift days and a loan from the Leswell Street Trust.

The plans were finalised and passed and work began with local builders Holloway & Connolly in charge of construction. The first phase was completed in time for the dedication service on Thursday 6th October 1994 when the Bishop of Worcester, the Right Rev. Philip Goodrich gave his blessing.

In the early 2,000s a second phase, costing £80,000, completed the main area with the addition of a new entrance hall, kitchen and cooking facilities. The Rev. Andi Jones returned in November 2002 to dedicate the work - she had been the first Vicar of St.Cecilia's.

More recently, in the autumn of 2008, the frontage was completed at a cost of £28,000. During the work the original 1912 foundation stone was exposed. It was carefully removed and now features as part of a new front wall.

St.Cecilia's, named after the lady who did so much for the church, now has its own DCC and a dedicated congregation with regular Sunday worship. The building has also become established as a meeting place for many organisations and a popular location for social events.

Quinquennial Inspection 1990 - still more problems

As required by the "Inspection of Churches Measure 1955" another Quinquennial Inspection of St.George's was completed in November 1990. The inspection was thorough and covered all aspects of the property, both buildings and grounds. The twenty-one-page report followed a survey made by architect David Mills. It acknowledged the work completed since a partial survey of 1985 and went on to highlight the continuing and worsening problems with the roof and its drainage. These will be explained later in the chapter.

Fellowship Area and more improvements

In 1991 the west end of the church was remodelled with the removal of some rear pews and the relocation of the Font to a position in-line with the south aisle pillars. These modifications prepared the way for the later construction of a new kitchen in the southwest corner and an enclosed storage area in the northwest corner. New panelled oak woodwork from the joinery shop of William Jackson Ltd. became a feature. In 1992, with the panelling complete, yet more pews were removed in order to create a new "Fellowship Area" at the west end of the church. This included a special children's area. The chancel and aisle carpets were now over sixty years old and a number of the town's companies were invited to quote for the replacement. The order was placed with Victoria Carpets Ltd. who, in 1993, wove a contract patterned Axminster in gold with a dark blue background. It was fitted by local carpet fitter T Jewkes.

The exteriors of the church also needed some attention. The windows in the north and south walls continued to be a target for the vandals and so, in 1993, faculties were issued for the addition of protective wire screening. The contract was given to H & R Developments of Redditch.

In the following year the tower was covered with scaffolding as Linford-Bridgeman Ltd. of Lichfield completed remedial and strengthening work on the ageing stonework. Some of the loose stones were removed and later sold.

A new 30-feet-high fibreglass flagpole was hoisted up the outside of the tower and manoeuvred into position by a team led by chorister Mike Pugh. A new St.George's flag was also purchased.

With this phase completed the Bishop of Worcester, the Right Rev. Philip Goodrich, performed an act of dedication on Sunday 8th October 1995.

The Rev. Hugh Anthony Burton BD. Team Vicar 1996 - 2008 Priest in Charge [Team Rector Designate] 2008 -

The Rev. Hugh Burton became Team Vicar in 1996 with special responsibilities for the daughter churches. He came from the village of Packington near Ashby-de-la-Zouch in the Leicester Diocese and moved, with his family, into the parish house in Comberton Avenue.

Hugh had good experience and in his formative years was a cathedral choirboy in the choir of Exeter Cathedral.

In Kidderminster he soon became popular as he cycled around the parish on his racing bicycle.

The Millennium photograph on the chancel steps

This traditional choir and clergy photograph was taken in November 2000. Front row - Mary Wyatt; the Rev. Caroline Windley, Curate; Norman Tatlow; the Rev. Nick Barker; Tim Morris; the Rev. Hugh Burton and Robin Burford. Behind them the assembled choir - too many in number to mention individually.

The Rev. Caroline Windley was the second female curate in the parish.

In 2008 Robina [Robin] Burford completed 25 years as a licensed reader.

Shortly after this photograph was taken the church was to have a face-lift.

Roof improvements, church redecoration & major organ restoratio

The 1983 roof problems in the northeast corner near the organ had been repaired and the associated problems with the organ had been dealt with but, in the following years, it was apparent that things were still not right in the organ loft. Therefore, in 1988 a further report was commissioned to assess these problems and, again, report on the condition of the roof in the vicinity of the organ. The report confirmed the worst fears and, in 1995, a more detailed survey suggested that major restoration work was now necessary on the roof and the organ!

Not daunted by the scale of the project or the potential cost it was decided to take the opportunity to follow on with a complete church interior redecoration programme. The work programme took time to arrange and finance.

Architect David Mills was called in to advise and supervise the work and so, in 1999 with the faculties in place, contracts were issued to W & S Long Ltd. of Wolverhampton to renew part of the chancel roof. The roof work was started in September 1999 and was complete by early 2000.

With the roof in good order Mark Silk and Neil Oakley of Interior Decor Ltd. Brierley Hill started the cleaning and redecoration work. One of the first jobs was to remove the Sanctuary east wall pelmet and red altar dorsal curtain together with two redundant vertical pipes. The Rector hired a special grinder for the latter exercise!

With a decision not to replace the curtain the DCC discussed the future decor for the east wall. Artist Richard Webb visited and made some proposals, a wooden cross, fixed to the wall was suggested but no firm decisions were made. It was eventually decided to leave the wall blank and paint it with a neutral colour - Dulux Buttermilk.

The main body of the church, with its high walls and extensive plasterwork, took some months to complete. Each Sunday the congregation was able to observe the progress as the portable tower scaffolding was moved around. The DCC had issued special instructions about the feet of the scaffolding in contact with the wooden floor and the new carpet!

Although not directly connected to the project it was an opportunity to improve the church's voice amplification system using state-of-art technology. In 1996 DCC member John Franklin spent many hours installing the wiring with connections to a control console near the west doors.

By far the most complex and expensive of the three jobs was the organ.

After considering all the alternatives, including a completely new electronic instrument, it was decided to rebuild the existing organ using a solid-state electro-pneumatic action coupled with a state-of-art console. Tim Morris drew up the final specification in consultation with John Bleney and Trevor Tipple who was another organ builder based in Worcester. With the final cost approaching £100,000 Trevor Tipple was awarded the contract.

While the roof repairs did not affect the Sunday worship the work on the organ was a different matter. It was a big job and took months to complete. A temporary freestanding electronic organ was positioned in the chancel and, for a time, the north stretch of nave seating was covered with organ parts and pipes. The reconditioned organ came back into service in July 2001.

It was an extensive period of expenditure and the church was now in good order as the Lord Bishop of Worcester, the Right Rev. Peter Selby dedicated the work on Sunday 16th September 2001.

In a celebration concert in December 2001 the organist of Gloucester Cathedral, David Briggs, attracted a large audience. He played music by J.S Bach, Mozart and others before attempting an impromptu composition with themes submitted by members of the audience during the interval.

Problems and security

It is sad to record that such a large church in isolation with an unwanted pathway cutting through continued to be an attraction for vandalism. While the main church windows were now protected the windows and the entrance to the annexe were not and this became the target in 2000.

To protect the property it was decided to enclose the annexe porch and improve the lighting around the church and annexe entrance. Church Warden Keith Mullard, a former employee of the Midland Electricity Board, used his contacts to obtain redundant concrete posts that had seen service in Rifle Range Road on Birchen Coppice Housing Estate. Leading a small team he installed the posts and security lights. For a short time a number of car thefts during the services prompted the DCC to take action and Geoff Holland purchased and installed a security camera linked to a television and recording unit in church. The camera viewed the main car parking area. The open church porch also became a home for vagrants and new wrought iron gates were made and installed by D Allum, Fabrications Ltd. They were dedicated to the memory of the popular the Rev. Leslie Guest and his wife Laura on Easter Sunday 2005.

After the Millennium

On a more positive note, the large illuminated Cross hanging from the west face of the tower has become a prominent town feature during darkness hours at the festive periods - again the work of Keith Mullard's team. Since the rededication, the organist maintained eye contact with the conductor and choir through a number of angled mirrors. In 2006 advancements in technology gave the ideal solution with the installation of a camera and closed circuit television system making the mirrors redundant. With the church building looking its best and a need to raise funds for the Restoration Fund a small group, led by Chris Tew, formed St.George's Concert Committee.

In the following years they organised a number of well-attended Saturday night concerts featuring a wide range of choral and instrumental music. Orchestras, choirs and soloists, hand-bell ringers all featured but, perhaps, the most popular for enthusiasts of the pipe organ were the organ recitals. Typical of these was the visit of Thomas Trotter, the Birmingham City Organist and International Soloist, who performed two concerts. No expense was spared as a large screen was positioned in the chancel projecting a view of the keyboards and foot pedals.

The rapid growth of mobile telephones brought requests to install transmission masts from the tower. Although potentially lucrative the requests were turned down by the DCC.

Church life continued with the Family Services, the annual Parish Service, the Alpha Course, the Parish Weekend and the ever-popular Easter Monday walk. The fortnightly Home Groups were well attended and the Annual Bereavement Service, generally held in October, gave the families of those who are not regular worshippers the opportunity to remember loved ones with the lighting of a remembrance candle. Boxes, filled with groceries, were donated and sent abroad to those in need.

Young people were well catered for with the CYFA Group. A number of young "Careforce" workers spent time working in the parish. For the younger generation there was "Pathfinders" and "Trekkers" and for the very young, "Parents and Toddlers". The annual Holiday Club was always a sell-out.

On Sunday 30th April 2006, after the morning service, Michael Hale, a former choirboy, launched his book "Hassocks & Cassocks, Ink-wells and School Bells" which charted his memories of life at St.George's Church and School.

"50 NOT OUT " was the title of a party at St.Cecilia's in September 2006 to celebrate 20 years' ministry by the Rev. Canon Nick Barker coupled with 30 years as Director of Music by Tim Morris. This proved to be one of the last parish events attended by the Barker family.

Over the years St.George's choir and congregation have provided good support for a number of local religious initiatives. These included the Diocesan Celebration of Faith at the Three Counties Showground in 1995 when the Archbishop of Canterbury visited; the Dedication of the town's Weavers' Wharf complex in 2005 and the Whitsunday Praise in the Park 2006 and 2007.

The end of an era

In 2007, after twenty-one years, the Rev. Canon Nick Barker left the parish to become Archdeacon of Auckland and Priest in Charge of Holy Trinity Darlington. His last services took place on Sunday 25th March 2007 with a special United Parish Communion in the morning that ended with the rousing Sousa march "Liberty Bell" commonly recognised as the Monty Python theme. In the evening, a Farewell Evensong was quieter with the Anthem "Blessed be the God and Father" and, at the conclusion, the choir sang John Rutter's anthem "The Lord bless you and keep you".

And so, in 2007, with an empty Rectory and parish in good order with all three churches looking their best, this history of St.George's comes to an end.

The Epilogue

After the Millennium

The Government's Church Building Act 1818 and its Waterloo Church investment was a resounding success. The selection of Kidderminster, with its growing population, was a popular decision and the criteria laid down at the time completely satisfied the local requirements.

It could also be argued that St.George's played its part as the growth of non-conformity was stemmed in the town and throughout the country.

Today, the church building is over 185 years old and since that time its landmark tower has looked down on a continuously changing town. The population is six times larger than when the church was built. The open fields surrounding the churchyard have become housing estates with established roads and a nearby park. People live longer and now have all the conveniences of modern living. Education is no longer the church's responsibility and the parish nurse is redundant. Traffic noise accompanies the services, jet aeroplanes fly overhead and mobile phones have to be turned off during the services.

In the town centre, the mills and carpet factories have been demolished making way for superstores and car parks and the building of the ring road has replaced most of the houses of a former congregation. The canal is part of the leisure industry and the town centre is for pedestrians only.

But the church building stands proud and unaffected by the years although it still retains the blackened external appearance sustained during the devastating fire coupled with the years of exposure to the industrial atmosphere of the town's carpet industry. However, the lofty interior is in good order and there is no better sight on a warm summer's day than to witness the sun streaming through the windows and picking out the colourful floral decorations so lovingly prepared.

In the foregoing chapters there have been many examples of the affection that individuals have retained for St.George's. Architect William Knight and the first Vicar of the parish were not from Kidderminster and yet they both chose to be buried close to the building they loved so much. William Villers set the standard and laid the foundation of tradition that remains to this day. But his church looked very different with its false ceiling, balcony and seating for 2000.
Over the years St.George's has been fortunate to have a succession of caring vicars and members of the congregation who have worked tirelessly to retain its fabric making it one of the foremost places of worship in the area. The church has a fine organ and the choir remains one of the best parish choirs in the diocese.

St. George's 2008

Today, St.George's is a large parish with many responsibilities both spiritual and financial. The Leswell Street Rectory is still the home of the incumbent, the Rev. Hugh Burton, who was licensed on 15th September 2008 with the title Priest in Charge [Team Rector Designate]. In the future the Diocese is planning to build a new Rectory in the grounds of the old one. It will be built to very high environmentally friendly standards in keeping with current concerns about climate change and our responsibility to be good stewards of God's earth. There are also plans to link with the parishes of Stone and Chaddesley Corbett.

Just under a quarter of the town's population live within the parish boundary and both daughter churches are playing their part attracting good congregations.

Over recent years the General Synod of the Church of England has had to contend with a number of controversial issues including the ordination of women to the priesthood, the gay issue and family considerations such as marriage in church, divorce and children out of wedlock. Locally, the Church Councils have become involved in the bureaucracy of modern culture with health and safety considerations, "no-smoking" signs, fire drills, job descriptions and the all important mission statement.

But life goes on and the future of St.George's is now in the hands of the current clergy and congregation who are the custodians during their years of service. However, change is inevitable and there will be some major decisions to be made in the years to come. Perhaps, those making the decisions will pause to read this book and remind themselves of the part that St.George's Church has played in the heritage of the town of Kidderminster.

Stop Press: On Sunday 28th June 2009 it was announced that *the Rev. Joseph Ayok-Loewenberg will become the next Vicar in St.George's Team Ministry. A native of Southern Sudan, he will come to the parish in August with his wife Karin and twin daughters.*

Appendix

Further information - people and donations

Curates in Charge

Years service in brackets

1824	W Villers [18]	1842	J Downall [5]	1847	T B Morrell [5]
1852	C J.M Mottram [15]				

Vicars and Rectors

1867	C J M Mottram [5*]	1872	F R Evans [4]	1876	S B Bathe [11]
1887	T W Church [28]	1915	A E R Bedford [3]	1918	R H Stephen [14]
1932	B J Isaac [13*]	1945	P J Martin [14*]	1959	L W Chidzey [10]
1969	E Montague-Youens [4]	1973	P D Chippendale [4]	1977	J R Ilson [9]
1986	N J W Barker [21]	2008	H A Burton		

* The Rev. C J M Mottram was in office a total of 20 years as curate in charge and vicar.
* The Rev. B J Isaac's war service took him from the parish leaving the Rev. P J Martin in control. This effectively reduced his time to 7 years and increased the Rev. Martin's to 20 years.

Curates of St.George's

A complete list of curates was not available at the time of publication.
The following names appear in the various documents and registers and represent a small selection - dates are approximate. Some of the later curates became Team Vicars.

1827 T Cook
1846 William Walsham How
1850 B Gibbons
1869 J L Chessire
1871 Charles P Mottram [son of C.J.M]
1873 Walter Wilmot Hill
1874 E Hobson
1875 W E Thompson
1876 Gerald Cokayne Vecqueray
1876 F J Cannon
1878 John Kingsmill C Key
1890 E J Barfeet
1890 Clement Ernest Newcomb
1896 Thomas R Glenn
1897 W Henderson
1900 Stanley Thomas
1900 George Martin
1900 T Fairfax Robson
1900 William Lea
1903 T F Stewart
1904 W Macintosh
1905 H Evans
1906 Edward W Bryan
1906 G E F Day
1914 F R J Easton
1919 B A Whitford
1924 William Frater Malcolm
1933 Noel Panter
1936 John William Fletcher Boughey
1939 Douglas Rene Tassell
1949 George Leslie Mallam
1950 Robert Rolls [Australian]
1950 G E Weaver
1958 Capt. R D Wisken

1960	G T Coombs	1974	A J [Jack] Mowate
1962	K [Ken] Griggs	1976	Edward Ffoulkes Williams
1964	Capt. David Ruddick	1978	Peter Williams
1964	Brian Shepherd	1978	Derek Little
1967	Capt. A Edge	1982	Michael Mitton
1967	Nigel Fox	1989	A [Andy] Piggott
1967	Henry John Smith	1994	Andrea [Andi] Jones
1970	Philip J W Darby	1997	Caroline Windley
1970	David J Bird	2001	Peter Huxtable

Also

Bert Hinton who served the church as a Licensed Reader before becoming ordained. After forty years service in the parish he left in 1983 to become Vicar of Rock.

Organists and Choirmasters

This list was compiled by Tim Morris from the old ledgers and is the best available.

1824 - 1828	Unrobed choir and small orchestra.	
1828 - 1832	Mr Manwill [4]	
1832 - 1833	George Hay [1]	Mr Grant choirmaster
1833 [1 month]	William Ward [1 month]	
1833	Mr Done [temporarily]	
1833 - 1855	Mr W.H Rogers [22]	
1840 ?	Mr Baldwin ?	
1850 - 1868	James Fitzgerald shared with St.Mary's [Dr. Marshall?]	
1868 - 1895	James Fitzgerald full time at St.George's [total 45]	
1896 ?	William Taylor formerly of Wribbenhall	
1895 - 1905	Edward M Chaundy [10]	
1905 - 1916	Richard A Taylor [11]	
1916 - 1921?	Henry William Radford [5?]	
1921? - 1926	Robert Edward Davies [5?]	
1926 - 1976	Harold Evers [50]	
1976 -	Timothy A Morris	

Members of the first choir in 1825

Samuel Kenny, James Ardney, Nathaniel Griffiths, Henry Price, John Shaw, Thomas Lench, Joseph Price, Charles Cooper, Benjamin Patton, Samuel Weston, Elizabeth Whitehouse, Mary Thomas, Margaret Lea, Elizabeth Barker, Phoebe Haywood, Charity Holloway, Thomas Hill and Samuel Cleevon.

Plaques, inscriptions and donations

Actual wording in italics.

Information taken from Church's Terrier and Inventory with assistance from Gordon Higgs. Other items added following a survey of the official records and the church.

Vestry location for use at services, some may have been donated.

* **Bowls, patens, dishes, plates, crosses, candlesticks, chalices, cruets, boxes, etc.**
* **Paten** engraved around top edge with "*IHS*" in centre. Inscribed under edge with "*L M T W Church, Vicar: 1887-1914 d.d MEC* " from 1972 Inventory.
* **Alms Dish** plain except for relief decoration on upper edge of dish. Engraved, "*Presented to St.George's Church, Kidderminster, in loving memory of Percy Groves May 1964* " from 1972 Inventory also number 4278.
* **Water Cruet** glass with silver stopper set in cork. Inscribed on silver band "*In loving memory of Miss May Fawcett. A founder member of the Soroptimists Club, Kidderminster. Died 1964* " from 1972 Inventory.
* **Water Cruet** glass with silver stopper set in cork. Stopper top in shape of a cross. Inscribed "*IHS 13th September 1925 " and "The Gift from the Girls Bible Class* " from 1972 Inventory.
* **Advent Ring** candle-holder made and donated by Mr. Bertram [Bert] Hinton
* **Consecration Medal** framed written on back.
  "*This medal was given by Mrs T W Church and presented by Mrs. Thomas Greenwood at the Centenary Bazaar February 1924 which was held in aid of the restoration of the Church after the disastrous fire. Mrs Greenwood gave the medal to the Church February 1945.* "
  Actual wording on medal "*THE FOUNDATIONS WERE BEGUN JULY XXI. AD. MDCCCXXI. THE CORONATION DAY OF HIS MAJESTY GEORGE IV. THE FIRST STONE WAS LAID THE XXVII DAY OF AUGUST IN THE SAME YEAR BY THE VENERABLE R F ONSLOW. MA. ARCHDEACON OF THE DIOCESE AND VICAR OF KIDDERMINSTER.*
  THE CHAPEL AND BURIAL GROUND WERE CONSECRATED THE XIII DAY OF SEPTEMBER AD. MDCCCXXIV. BY THE RIGHT REVEREND F.H.W CORNWALL DD. LORD BISHOP OF WORCESTER.
  THE EXPENSE OF ERECTING THIS CHAPEL WAS DEFRAYED PARTLY BY A GRANT FROM PARLIAMENT UNDER ACTS PASSED IN THE 58 & 59 YEARS OF GEORGE 3 AND PARTLY BY A VOLUNTARY SUBSCRIPTION OF 2000£ FROM THE INHABITANTS OF THE TOWN & NEIGHBOURHOOD OF KIDDERMINSTER.
  IT CONTAINS 2000 SITTINGS OF WHICH 1200 ARE APPROPRIATED TO THE ACCOMMODATION OF THE POOR & IT IS BUILT UPON A SITE WHICH TOGETHER WITH A SPACIOUS BURIAL GROUND ADJOINING WAS PROVIDED AT THE EXPENSE OF THE PARISH.
  FRANCIS GOODWIN, ARCHITECT "
* **Altar Service Book** "*Presented to St.George's Church Kidderminster on the rededication September 13, 1925 by Mary Evelyn Edwards* "
* **Altar Service Book** [see above] "*Presented by her daughter on 1st June 1962 to St.George's Church Kidderminster in memory of Mary Evelyn Edwards to replace the Altar Book which she gave to the church on its rededication 13 September 1925* ".

* **Book of Common Prayer** "*To the Glory of God and in memory of Ina Anderson. Presented to St.George's Church, Parish Kidderminster, September 1962* ".
* **The Prayer Book as proposed 1928** "*Presented by N & H.F Thorneloe in memory of Major H Thorneloe and family who worshipped at St.George's + Requiscant in Pace* ".
* **Holy Bible** "*Presented by St.George's Mothers Union Branch for use in All Saint's Chapel* " signed "*Joyce H Smith. Enrolling Member* ".
* **Church Plate in the Archdeaconry of Worcester** book with diagrams "*Given to the Vicar of St.George's, Kidderminster by Marian S Church. January 1915* " written under "*Returned to the present Vicar by the widow of a former Churchwarden in 1950 and deposited by him in the Churchwardens Chest. October 1950* " signed "*PJM [Rev. P.J Martin] 3/10/50 - for St.George's plate see pages 39 & 40* ".
* **Holy Bible** handwritten inside cover "*Mrs Chell, a gift from her children, Mary & Ellen, their reward from the Stourport Church Sunday School, Michaelmas, 1888* "
* **Candle snuffer** on short pole
* **Manger and Christmas figures** made and donated by Keith Mullard

North Wall

* **Plaque list of curates and vicars** *Names and dates only as shown earlier.*
  Note: This plaque was originally installed on the West wall near the doors. It was relocated when the oak panelling was added.
* **Rededication plaque**
  "*This Church was consecrated on September 13, 1824 by the Right Reverend, F H W Cornewall DD Lord Bishop of Worcester. The interior was destroyed by fire on November 20, 1922. The restored Church was Rededicated by the Right Reverend E H Pearce Litt.D. DD CBE Lord Bishop of Worcester September 13, 1925. G G Scott RA Architect for Restoration; R H Stephen MA Vicar; H C Rhodes, J B S Robinson Churchwardens* ".
  Note: This plaque was originally installed on the West wall near the doors. It was relocated when the oak panelling was added.
* **Charles Harvey Memorial plaque** stone in north west alcove
  "*To the Glory of God and in memory of Charles Harvey. This tablet has been dedicated by friends who Desire to preserve the memory of A true Son of the Church of England who Loved the place where God's Honour Dwelleth* ".

* **Flags** - 4 flags held in a stand.
  "*Kidderminster Boy Scouts* " - dark blue and red
  "*3rd Kidderminster, St George's - Be prepared* "- green
  "*3rd Kidderminster, St George's Wolf Cubs - Do your best* " - yellow
  "*British Legion, Kidderminster Branch* "- dark blue

Sanctuary Area

* **Altar frontal, dorsals and fair linin** presented in memory of Elizabeth Barratt, dedicated October 1971
* **Altar frontal** presented by Sidney [Sid] James in memory of his wife Linda and her mother.
* **Bishops Chair** carved wooden chair with crest.
* **Chairs** two carved matching chairs.

* **T.W Church presentation chair** carved with brass plaque on upper backrest. "*Presented to the Rev. Theobald W Church by the members of St.Mary's Young Men's Bible Class, October 1887* ".
* **Banner** no title "*Children of St.George's* "
* **Flower stand** in wrought iron with brass plaque. "*In affectionate memory of Dorothy Powell, dedicated leader of St.George's Young Wives Group* ".
* **Clergy seat and desk** oak with brass plaque. "*To the Glory of God and in loving memory of Pollie Pardoe for more than sixty years a devoted worker and faithful worshipper in this church - 19 October 1885-5th May 1978. Always remembered by her family* ".
* **Clergy seat and desk** oak [same design as above] inscription carved on side "*To the Glory of God and in loving memory of Lillian Maud Fawcett who worshipped in this church and, though blind, taught for over 50 years in the Sunday School* ".
* **Carpet in Sanctuary** brass plaque on choir vestry wall "*This Sanctuary carpet was presented by Edith Gethin to mark the faithful and devoted service rendered to the church as Churchwardens by her father-in-law, her husband and her son. Henry Westbury Gethin. Harry Mansell Gethin. Basil Harry Gethin* ".
* **Table / stand for cross behind altar** brass plaque "*To the Glory of God and in loving memory of Eva Dugarde Greenhill. September 1964* "
* **Stained glass Rose Window** brass plaque on wall. "*The Peace Window. The stained glass in the Rose Window was donated by Miss May Parker and dedicated to the Glory of God by the Bishop of Worcester. 5th June 1988* ".
* **Altar Candlesticks** a pair of brass candlesticks presented by Miss Muriel Robinson in memory of her parents Joseph and Sophia Robinson [stolen in 1975].
* **Wooden Altar Cross** made and donated by the Rev. Peter Chippendale, hand written and signed on base "*St.George's Church Kidderminster, Easter 1975. Peter D Chippendale* ".
* **Altar Candlesticks** a pair of brass candlesticks with turned wooden bases, brass plaque on base "*St.George's Church in loving memory of my dear parents Annie Allen 1879-1961, Frederick Allen 1878-1968. Presented and made by Arthur - only son 1975* ".

Chancel Area

* **Pulpit** carved oak with brass plaque "*To the Glory of God and in memory of those who formerly worshipped in this church and have passed onward. this pulpit was given by Emma M Morgan.* "
* **Pulpit light** brass plaque inside pulpit "*This Pulpit light was presented to the church by Mr H M Jeffery in memory of his niece Heather Barbara Loney who passed away November 7th 1950, aged 17 years. Dedicated by the Rt. Rev. R S Fyffe late Bishop of Rangoon on April 22nd 1951*".
* **Eagle Lectern** carved oak with brass plaque "*To the Glory of God and in memory of William J Thompson. The gift of Annie Thompson. Dedicated September 13th. 1936.* "
* **Clergy seat and desk** carved oak with brass plaque. Decani "*To the Glory of God and in loving memory of Walter Hill for over sixty years a faithful worker for the church in this parish. September 1964.* "
* **Clergy seat and desk** carved oak with brass plaque. Cantori "*To the Glory of God and in loving memory of William Charles Pardoe for many years a faithful member of this church. Presented by his loving wife Pollie Pardoe. September 1964.* "

* **Plain portable Lectern** oak with brass plaque
"*Presented to St.George's Church in loving memory of Edith Gethin 1886-1971 by her three sons - Basil, Aubrey and Rex Gethin members of P.C.C for 60 years and hon. secretary 1941-47* "
* **Lectern falls** - four falls in Red, Oatmeal, Purple and Green donated by Barry & Melvyn Thompson in memory of their mother Doris H.M Thompson 1981
* **Choir Screens** Decani brass plaque on choir screen. Presented by Ernest Hawkes 1963
"*These choir screens were erected and dedicated to the Glory of God and in loving memory of George Henry Randall Chorister of this church 1894 - 1945 and his sister Sarah Annie Hawkes a member of this church 1897 - 1945. LAUS DEO*".
* **Decani Reading desks** brass plaque rear choir stall
"*The rear reading desks were donated in memory of Bernard [Barney] Everard* ".
* **Decani Candle holders** brass plaque front choir stall
"*The candle holders were donated in memory of Geoffrey William Bell* ".
* **Cantori Reading desks** brass plaque front choir stall
"*The front reading desks were donated in memory of Walter J [Bob] Scott* ".
* **Cantori Candle holders** brass plaque rear choir stalls
"*The candle holders were donated in memory of Frederick Victor [Vic] Summers* ".
* **Grand Piano brass plaque** on front
"*To the Glory of God and in memory of Henry Arthur Morris. presented by his loving wife Mary* "
* **Decani Urn** - Bath stone with carved inscription.
"*Helen Maud Brown Archibald Willie Brown* "
* **Cantori Urn** - Bath stone with carved inscription.
"*Vera Kathleen Summers Frederick Victor Summers* "

Choir vestry, organ

* **Framed picture** over lockers
Printed title "*Christus in Gethsemane* ". Hand written and signed by former organist "*To the Glory of God and in thankful remembrance of years 1905-1916. R A Taylor* ".
* **T.W Church Vestry** - carved stone over main choir vestry door
"*To the Glory of God and in loving memory of Theobald W Church MA Vicar of this Parish from July 1887 to December 1914. This Choir Vestry replaces the Memorial Vestry erected by Parishioners and Friends, which was destroyed by fire on November 20th 1922* "
* **Organ case dedication** carved stone plaque near entrance to choir vestry
"*To the Glory of God the organ case and west display was erected by public donation in memory of Gerald Kenneth Morris JP FRICS 1923-1982* ".
* **Processional Cross** fixed to end of choir stalls - brass plaque
"*In memory of Phyllis May Humphries* "
* **Royal School of Church Music plaque**
Over entrance to choir vestry, presented by Bernard [Barney] Everard former chorister.

Nave Area

* **Stone Font on wooden base and cover** brass plaque
"*To the memory of William & Ellen Brown, James & Catherine Coates for many years devoted worshippers in this church. Erected by Archibald W & Helen Brown* ".
* **Candleholder stand** near font
"*In loving memory of John S Harris 1929 - 1994* ".

* **Oak Bookcase** freestanding with brass plaque
"To the Glory of God and in loving memory of Arthur Norman Gwillam 1918 - 96. Life long member of this church and late Headmaster of St.George's & Offmore Schools. Always remembered by his loving wife Gwen and sons Roy and John & his family ".

* **Large book holder and table-top** near west doors
"To the Glory of God and in memory of Ivy May and Percy Knowles whose legacy provided this book holder and new amplification system ".

* **2 Hymn boards** brass plaque - former chorister
"In loving memory of Hugh Ernest Jones, January 21st 1965 ".

* **2 Hymn Boards** original from rededication. Possibly donation George Law 1909.

* **2 Warden staves** wooden carving by Mr Pancheri of Bromsgrove. Donated by Muriel Robinson in memory of her parents

* **2 Warden staves** black with brass orb and cross.

* **8 Offertory plates** turned wood.

* **Flower stand** in store
"In memory of Ernest Meredith 1891-1969 ".

* **Flower stand** in store
"In memory of Alfred John Wilson 1903-1982. Lillian and Lyndon Hendrickson USA ".

* **Flower stand** in store - J.B Robinson was the warden at the 1925 rededication
"In loving memory of Joseph Benjamin Robinson for many years churchwarden of St.George's Parish Church and his wife Ellen Sophia Robinson. His servants shall serve him ".

* **Flower stand** in store
"In affectionate memory of Dorothy Powers a dedicated leader of St.George's Young Wives Group. "

South Wall

* **Key memorial** diamond shaped stone plaque in All Saint's Chapel area
"In memory of Charlotte Key daughter of Sir Kingsmill Grove Key Bart. and sister of the Rev'd John Kingsmill C Key MA. She was for 3 years a Sunday School teacher and earnest church-worker in the Parish and was suddenly called away from earth on the day before she intended to set sail to work with her brother for the Central African Mission in Zanzibar. October 26, 1881".
[The Rev. Key was a curate at St.George's]

* **Bathe memorial** plaque on brass, wood with glass cover in All Saint's Chapel area
"To the Glory of God and in memory of Stephen Brown Bathe MA of Balliol College, Oxford, Rector of Rusbury, Salop who died at Bath on 5th day of June 1891, aged 49 years. This tablet is erected in grateful recollection of his devoted pastoral work, unfailing kindness and ready sympathy with all in trouble while Vicar of this Parish from October 1876 to July 1887 ".

* **Amplification memorial** stone plaque with carved lettering. Presented by Mrs M Stradling 1963

"*To the Glory of God and in loving memory of Gertrude Louisa Pritchard, Anne Rew Pritchard and Eugine Stradling. The amplification system in this church was presented by Minnie Latham Stradling with gratitude for loving parents and husband. September 22, 1963* ".

Note: This plaque was originally installed near the West Doors. It was relocated when the oak panelling was installed.

* **Sir George Eddy Bell ringing memorial** stone plaque with carved lettering

"*To the Glory of God and in thanksgiving for a long life of happiness and public service the six bells and hymn-playing mechanism in this church was presented by Alderman Sir George Eddy OBE JP [Honorary Freeman of Kidderminster] Mayor 1922, 1928, 1936 and Coronation Year 1937 in celebration of his eighty fifth birthday, June 22nd 1963, unveiled by Bishop of Worcester* ".

West Wall

* **Warden memorial plaque** north alcove carved lettering

"*In loving memory of James Creswell Walker, Vicar's Warden of this parish who died August 14th 1924 aged 69 years. The tablet was erected by his widow* "

* **Porch gates** brass plaque near west doors

"*To the Glory of God the porch gates were erected in memory of the Rev. Leslie Guest and his wife Laura, much loved in their ministry in this parish and district for over 50 years, 2004* ".

Southeast All Saints' Chapel

* **Stained Glass window** plaque behind altar curtain

"*The window above this plate was erected in 1929 in memory of Good Mothers* "

* **Banner** freestanding

"*St.George's M U Kidderminster* "

* **Cross and candlesticks memorial** brass plaque on credence table/shelf

"*To the Glory of God and in memory of her parents John and Blanche Garlick - the brass cross and candlesticks used in this chapel were given by their daughter Shelia, January 2008* ".

Northeast Chapel Area

* **Altar table** memorial brass plaque

"*In remembrance of Mum, Florence May Cowdry, from her loving children.* "

* **T Holden HMS Kite** memorial brass plaque on memorial

"*In memory of A/B T F Holden of this Parish also 216 shipmates who died with him on 21 August 1944. If blood be the price of Admiralty, Lord God we have paid in full* ".

Annexe

* **Annexe opening** dedication plaque entrance to annex building

"*St.George's Church Annexe - dedicated by the Rt. Rev. Robin Woods K.C.V.O MA, Lord Bishop of Worcester. Opened by The Ven Christopher R Campling MA, Archdeacon of Dudley.
17th July 1981. Arch: H.W Rolley RIBA   Cont: George Law Ltd.
Vicar Rev. John Ilson BSC DD, Church wardens A.E Carter, N.H Tatlow* ".

* **Kitchen equipment** was dedicated to the memory of Harold Evers.

Other benefactors and Trusts

* **Main [Angel gates] and side gates** manufactured and donated by Bert Hinton 1961.

* **Lectern Bible** large with New English Bible with Apocrypha - hand written
"*This Lectern Bible is presented to St.George's Church Kidderminster and in loving memory of Doris May Millward. 1976* "

* **Lectern Bible** large on Memorial chapel altar
"*This Lectern Bible was presented to St.George's Parish Church, Kidderminster by Sir George & Lady Eddy on the occasion of Sir George's eighty-sixth birthday. June 22nd 1966. Laus Deo* ".

* **Pew Bibles** bound Good News bibles undated
"*Northfield Trust - The Gift of Doctor John Hall late Bishop of Bristol.* "

* **Collection of Anthems** former chorister Neville Smart
"*An Anthem Anthology for St.George's Church Kidderminster. Selected by Neville Smart [Benefactor & former chorister].* "

* **Collection of Anthems** by former chorister Harry Long
"*Collection of Anthems presented to St.George's Church Kidderminster by Mr Harry Long, June 1957* ".

* **Collection of Anthems** by former chorister Geoff Bell
"*Severn Anthems, Edward Elgar. Donated to the Choir of St.George's Church in Memory of Harold Evers (Orgainst & Choirmaster 1926-1976) by G W Bell Esq.* "

* **The McFarlane Trust** - Bob McFarlane former chorister. Wife Mary wrote - "*To the Vicar and Churchwardens of St.George's Church Kidderminster as a fund to enable them to purchase hymn books, prayer books, bibles, cassocks and surplices for the benefit of the Choir of which my husband was a member for forty years* ".

* **Leswell Street Trust** set up with income from the sale of Leswell Street School.

* **Earthenware [terracotta] dish** made in sections - Ladies Fellowship with Annette Christopher. "*St.George's Fellowship Kidderminster 19.5.06* "

* **Kneelers** - members of the congregation made a number of kneelers from materials supplied by Jackson's of Hebdon Bridge, West Yorkshire. On some the name of the maker and to whom they are dedicated. Sheila Garlick; Kathleen Turk; Doris Burrows; Doris Burrows "*to Frank Burrows 1917-1983* "; Doris Burrows "*to Lewis my son* "; Mrs P.M Turner [nee Fidoe] "*dedicated to Sgt. T S Fidoe* "; Mrs P M Turner "*to the fallen of this Parish*"; Elsie Westwood, worked by Pam Upsall "*dedicated to John Westwood* "; Vickey Higgs "*Sarah's Confirmation* "; Joy Crosher "*dedicated to John Franklin, Church Warden* ".
Some are dated 1995.

* **Banners** - a number of banners have been made by the ladies of the congregation.
Large west balcony banner "*I am the vine - You are the branches* " by Julie Varey, Joy Crosher, Pam Upsall, Patricia Peck and Barbara Everett.
Others titles - "*Fruits of the Spirit* ", "*Nativity* ", "*St.George's Choir* ", "*Stars of Betheleham* ", "*John 10 v 10* ", "*Hebrews 10 v 23* ", "*Isiah 43 vs 18/19* ", "*Easter* ", "*Rise & Shine and give God the Glory* ", "*I Will Pour Out My Spirit* ". All made by small groups made up from the following - Judith Hill, Margaret White, Marguerite Clarke, Julie Varey, Marjorie Nelson, Freda Brugsch, Christina Bytheway and Sheila Hobson.
The Friday Morning Group at Chris Griffith's house - Lisa and Kathryn Manser, Rosemary Knott, Julie Varey and Sarah Grimshore.
Also, St.George's Trekkers.

Year Book accounts 1936

ST. GEORGE'S PAROCHIAL CHURCH COUNCIL ACCOUNTS.

1936.

Receipts.	£ s. d.	£ s. d.
Credit Balance in Bank		19 9 1
Offertories :—		
Duplex ...	194 2 10	
Loose Cash ...	248 7 6	
		442 10 4
Special Collections :—		
Mothers Union Mar. 11 ...	7 6	
Mothers Union Dec. 9 ...	7 6	
Waifs and Strays	11 0	
Old Boys' Service	1 3 6	
Sunday School Treat Whit-Sunday	7 11	
Sunday School Treat Whit-Monday	1 0 0	
Missionary Sunday (C.M.S.) ...	6 5 0	
Confirmation Service (The Bishop's fund)	1 14 0	
St. Dunstan's ...	2 2 6	
		13 18 11
Lentern Boxes		2 16 6
Church Rate		6 17 0
Pew Rents		43 5 6
Charities :—		
Little's Charity ...	3 17 0	
Miss Meredith's Legacy ...	17 2 6	
Mrs. Morgan's Legacy	8 14 8	
Charles Lawley's Legacy ...	4 16 10	
		34 11 0
Vicar's returned Easter offering		5 0 0
Profits on Socials :—		
Winter Social	16 5 0	
Garden Fête	140 18 3	
Bridge Drive	33 17 6	
		191 0 9
Insurance for Boiler		8 5 0
Grant from St. Andrews :—		
For Diocesan Quota	10 0 0	
For Add. Clergy Fund	5 0 0	
		15 0 0
Special Donation		1 0 0
Total		£783 14 1

Expenditure.	£ s. d.
Parish Clerk	85 0 0
Parish Room Cleaner ...	15 0 0
Church Cleaning	2 0 0
Coke	42 14 3
Laundry	5 0 2
Organist	60 0 0
Choir Boys	16 0 0
Choir Outing	15 0 0
Music	7 9 1
Organ Tuning	8 8 0
Duplex	15 0 0
Duplex Equipment	1 17 8
Rates	1 7 0
Tithe	1 4
Repairs	2 12 3
Printing and Advertising ...	12 16 0
Stationery and Books ...	4 1 7
Electric Supply	25 16 8
Electric Fitments and Repairs	5 10 2
Commission on Pew Rents ...	1 15 10
Insurances	33 18 0
Lawley Charity (for the poor)	4 16 10
Nursing Association ...	17 2 6
Churchyard Sec.	8 14 8
Schools' Maintenance ...	40 0 0
Sunday Schools	14 0 0
Sunday School Treat ...	1 7 11
Day School Prizes	5 0 0
Archdeacons Visitation ...	16 0
Bread and Wine	5 19 10
Vicar's Easter Offering ...	30 2 0
Vicar in lieu of Pew Rents ...	50 0 0
General Hospital	10 0 0
Diocesan Quota	85 0 0
Missionary Efforts	15 3 2
Waifs and Strays	11 0
Earl Haigs Fund	2 0 0
St. Dunstan's	2 2 6
Cheque Book	10 0
Sundries	3 3 3
Curate's Stipend	19 0 0
Postages	19 1
Diocesian Messengers ...	4 1 0
Deaf and Dumb Institution ...	1 1 0
C. of E. Empire Settlement ...	5 0
The Bishop's Fund	1 14 0
Licencing fee	13 0
Faculty fees	5 17 2
Floral Wreaths	1 2 6
Pew Seating	38 7 0
Mother's Union Secretary ...	15 0
Additional Clergy Fund ...	5 0 0
	736 12 5
Credit Balance 31st Dec., 1936	45 11 8
Cash in Hand	1 10 0
Total	£783 14 1

C. J. VINEY,
T. R. BADLAND, *Churchwardens.*

H. COOK,
W. G. GETHIN, *Auditors.*

2

ST. ANDREW'S CHURCHWARDENS'. ACCOUNTS.

1936.

Receipts.	£ s. d.
General Offertory	55 4 4
Freewill Offering	2 16 0
Restoration Fund	11 5 0
Sale of Harvest produce ...	14 0
Lenten Offerings	7 12 9
Balance in Bank Dec. 31st, 1935	31 6 7
	£108 8 8

Expenditure.	£ s. d.
Caretaker	13 0 0
National Health Insurance ...	4 6 8
Organist, Blower, Choir Boys and Bellringer	23 16 5
Gas, Mantles, Coal and Coke...	6 11 10
Care of Churchyard	3 5 0
Harvest Festival Bills ...	7 0
Fire Insurance	1 10 0
Music 25/- A/c book 4/- ...	1 9 0
The Vicar (Easter Offering)	2 0 0
Diocesan Quota	15 0 0
Organ Tuning	2 10 0
Water Rates	12 0
Grant to Choir Outing ...	2 2 6
Cheque Book	10 0
Chain and Locks	3 4
Laundry (Curtains)	10 0
Cruet	17 9
Balance in Bank Dec. 31st. 1936	30 7 2
	£108 18 8

Mr. J. THATCHER,
Mrs. EDWARDS, *Churchwardens.*

Examined and found correct,
WILLIAM C. PARDOE, *Auditor.*

JOHN HUMPHREY'S CHARITY.

(FABRIC ACCOUNT).

Receipts.	£ s. d.
Jan. 1 Balance	9 4 0
,, 24 G.W.R. Dividend ...	9 8 0
July 24 ,, ,, ...	9 8 0
Dec. 31 Bank Interest ...	5 9
	£28 5 9

Expenditure.	£ s. d.
Oct. 23 Repairs, Messrs. Dudley	6 12 6
Dec. 15 Ecclesiastical Insurance	10 0 0
,, 31 Credit Balance ...	11 13 3
	£28 5 9

C. J. VINEY,
T. R. BADLAND, *Churchwardens.*

Examined and found correct,
H. COOK,
W. G. GETHIN. *Auditors.*

ADDITIONAL CLERGY FUND.

Receipts.	£ s. d.
Jan. 1 Balance in hand ...	24 15 3
,, 21 Cheque from St. Andrews	5 0 0
Apr. 22 Conversion Loan Dividend	10 14 1
,, 29 Vicar's Cheque (from Curate's Fund) ...	9 11 5
Oct. 22 Conversion Loan Dividend	10 14 1
,, 29 Vicar's Cheque (from Curate's Fund) ...	3 19 6
Dec. 31 Bank Interest ...	2 1
	£64 16 5

Expenditure.	£ s. d.
Jan. 27 Curates Stipend ...	29 8 4
July 13 Curates Stipend ...	20 8 4
Dec. 31 Credit Balance ...	14 19 9
	£64 16 5

C. J. VINEY,
T. R. BADLAND, *Churchwardens.*

Examined and found correct,
H. COOK,
W. G. GETHIN, *Auditors.*

3

ST. GEORGE'S GARDEN FETE.

Held at Fairlawn, Comberton, July 1st, 1936.

Receipts.	£	s.	d.	Expenditure.	£	s.	d.
Vicarage Stall	47	0	0	Hire of Tents, etc.	9	0	0
Refreshment Stall	31	2	0	Erection of Stalls, hire of Chairs, etc	9	0	0
Selfridges Stall	20	0	0	Music (Radiogram)	3	10	0
Produce Stall	19	5	4	Printing—F. R. Bennett ...	1	5	0
Ices Stall	9	15	8	Messrs. Cheshire ...	1	4	6
Sweet Stall	4	8	9	Kidder. Shuttle ...		13	6
Hoop-la Stall	3	14	0	Advertising- ,, ,, ...		12	0
Taken at Dancing Displays	2	3	7	,, Times ...		2	6
Bean Board & Bagatelle ...	2	0	0	Billposting Co.		12	6
Skittles .. ,, ...	1	10	10	Clearing up Grounds ...		5	0
Infant School Doll	2	1	8	Balance Profit	140	18	3
Air Gun Shooting	1	4	8				
Clock Golf		18	3				
American Bowls		9	8				
Taken at Dolls House ...		9	4				
Sale of Programmes ...		14	4				
Bottle of Peas (guessing) ...		7	3				
Dart Throwing		4	5				
Taken at Gate	7	0	0				
Sale of Tickets	5	18	0				
Donations	6	15	6				
	£167	3	3		£167	3	3

Examined and found correct,
W. G. FISHER.

C. J. VINEY,
T. R. BADLAND, *Churchwardens & Joint Secs.*

ST. GEORGE'S & HOOBROOK SCHOOLS MAINTENANCE A/C.

Receipts.	£	s.	d	Expenditure.	£	s.	d.
Jan. 1 Balance brought forward	11	5	1	Jan. 23 Ivens, Morton & Morton Insurance ...	12	3	0
21 Churchwardens ...	20	0	0	23 Cheshires, Stationery...		8	6
Mar. 3 ,, ...	20	0	0	Feb. 14 Brain. J. H., Painting a/c Hoobrook ...	15	18	0
				Mar. 6 Education Committee	10	0	0
				11 Brain, J. H., Repairs	1	14	11
				Apr. 21 Ivens, Morton & Morton Insurance ..	3	3	9
				Dec. 22 Brain, J. H., Repairs	2	6	0
				31 Balance in Bank ...	5	10	11
	£51	5	1		£51	5	1

A. W. BROWN, Hon. Sec. & Treas.

Examined and found correct,
JOSH B S. ROBINSON.

WORCESTER CROSS SCHOOLS CAPITAL ACCOUNT.

Receipts.	£	s.	d.	Expenditure.	£	s.	d.
Jan. 1 Balance in Bank ...	37	2	4	Dec. 31 Credit Balance ...	37	13	3
June 30 Bank Interest ...		5	6				
Dec. 31 ,, ,, ...		5	5				
	£37	13	3		£37	13	3

C. J. VINEY,
T. R. BADLAND, *Churchwardens*

Examined and found correct,
H. COOK,
W. G. GETHIN. *Auditors.*

ORGAN FUND.

Receipts.	£	s.	d.	Expenditure.	£	s.	d.
Jan. 1 Balance in hand ...	30	16	3	Dec. 31 Credit Balance ...	46	6	5
Feb 18 Donation	1	2	0				
June 26 ,, ...	1	15	0				
Nov. 30 Transferred from Font Fund	11	3	6				
,, 30 Donation	1	0	0				
Dec. 31 Bank Interest ...		9	8				
	£46	6	5		£46	6	5

C. J. VINEY,
T. R. BADLAND, *Churchwardens.*

Examined and found correct,
H. COOK,
W. G. GETHIN, *Auditors.*

ST. GEORGE'S YOUNG MENS' CLUB.

Receipts.	£	s.	d.	Expenditure.	£	s.	d.
Balance Sept. 1936 ...	3	6	9	A. Preedy & Sons ...	3	17	2
Takings by Games, Cigarettes and Subscriptions ...	26	17	3	Thos. Padmore & Sons ...	6	2	0
				League Fees	2	14	0
				Catering per S. Dearne ...	1	14	0
				Gas Company	1	9	0
				General Rates	1	4	6
				F. R. Russell		17	6
				F. R. Bennett (Printing) ...		12	0
				Cleaning, Firewood, Postages as per Secretary's Account	5	13	2
				Money Order Charges ...		4	6
				Sundries		2	0
				Cash at Lloyds Bank ...	3	0	0
				,, ,, Co-op. ,, ...	1	10	0
				,, in Treasurer's Hands ...	1	4	2
	£30	4	0		£30	4	0

T. C. SPILSBURY, Secretary.

W. BENNETT, Treasurer.

ST. GEORGE'S YOUNG MENS' CLUB, LOAN A/C.

Receipts.	£	s.	d.	Expenditure.	£	s.	d.
Jan. 1 Credit Loan 1935 ...	13	0	0	Dec. 31 Loan Balance ...	13	0	0
	£13	0	0		£13	0	0

Examined and found correct,
H. COOK,
W. G. GETHIN,

C. J. VINEY,
T. R. BADLAND, *Churchwardens.*

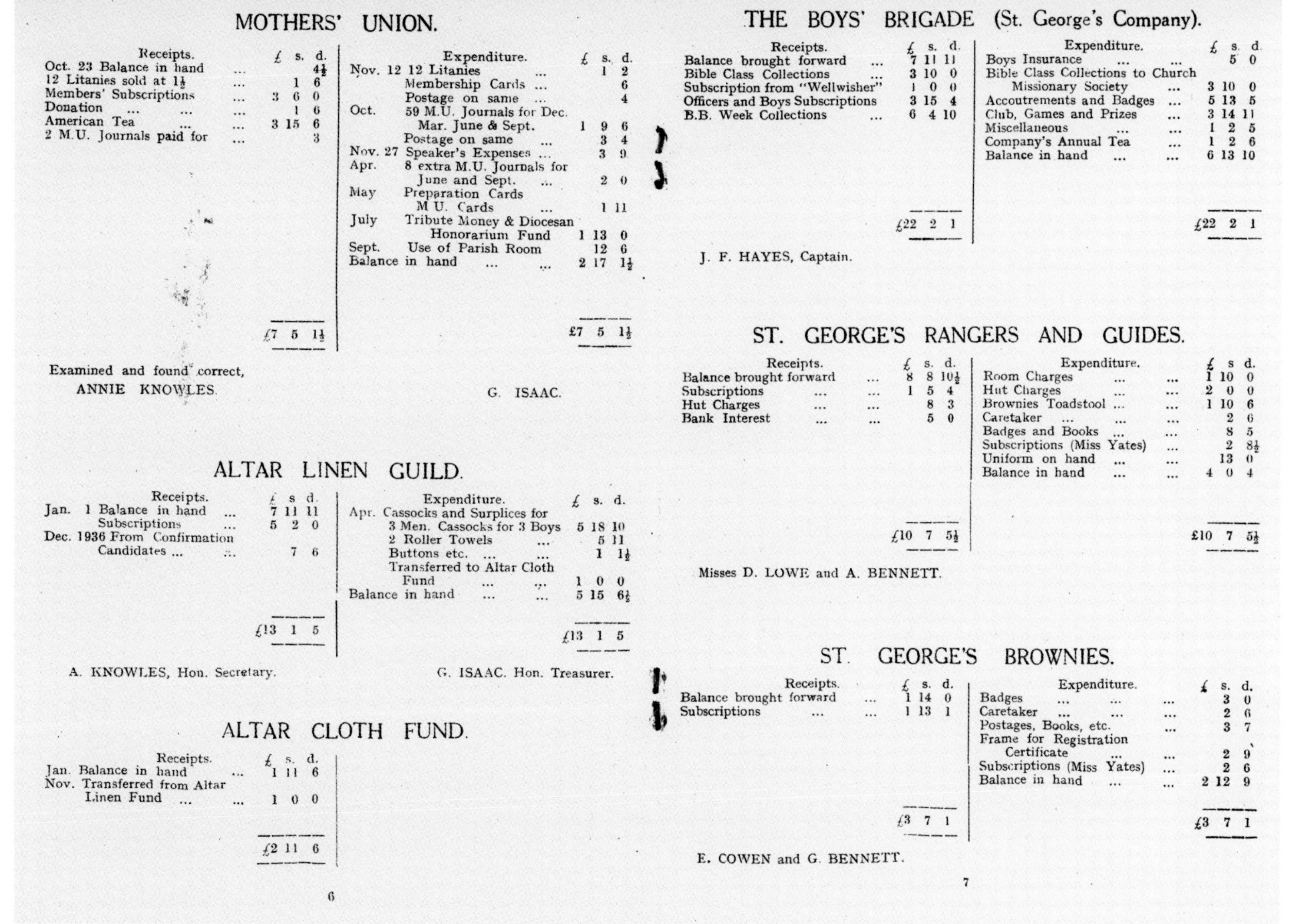

MOTHERS' UNION.

Receipts.	£	s.	d.
Oct. 23 Balance in hand ...			4½
12 Litanies sold at 1½ ...		1	6
Members' Subscriptions ...	3	6	0
Donation		1	6
American Tea	3	15	6
2 M.U. Journals paid for ...			3
	£7	5	1½

Expenditure.	£	s.	d.
Nov. 12 12 Litanies ...		1	2
Membership Cards ...			6
Postage on same ...			4
Oct. 59 M.U. Journals for Dec. Mar. June & Sept.	1	9	6
Postage on same ...		3	4
Nov. 27 Speaker's Expenses ...		3	9
Apr. 8 extra M.U. Journals for June and Sept. ...		2	0
May Preparation Cards M.U. Cards ...		1	11
July Tribute Money & Diocesan Honorarium Fund	1	13	0
Sept. Use of Parish Room		12	6
Balance in hand	2	17	1½
	£7	5	1½

Examined and found correct,
ANNIE KNOWLES.

G. ISAAC.

ALTAR LINEN GUILD.

Receipts.	£	s.	d.
Jan. 1 Balance in hand ...	7	11	11
Subscriptions ...	5	2	0
Dec. 1936 From Confirmation Candidates		7	6
	£13	1	5

Expenditure.	£	s.	d.
Apr. Cassocks and Surplices for 3 Men. Cassocks for 3 Boys	5	18	10
2 Roller Towels ...		5	11
Buttons etc.		1	1½
Transferred to Altar Cloth Fund	1	0	0
Balance in hand	5	15	6½
	£13	1	5

A. KNOWLES, Hon. Secretary.

G. ISAAC. Hon. Treasurer.

ALTAR CLOTH FUND.

Receipts.	£	s.	d.
Jan. Balance in hand ...	1	11	6
Nov. Transferred from Altar Linen Fund	1	0	0
	£2	11	6

6

THE BOYS' BRIGADE (St. George's Company).

Receipts.	£	s.	d.
Balance brought forward ...	7	11	11
Bible Class Collections ...	3	10	0
Subscription from "Wellwisher"	1	0	0
Officers and Boys Subscriptions	3	15	4
B.B. Week Collections ...	6	4	10
	£22	2	1

Expenditure.	£	s.	d.
Boys Insurance		5	0
Bible Class Collections to Church Missionary Society ...	3	10	0
Accoutrements and Badges ...	5	13	5
Club, Games and Prizes ...	3	14	11
Miscellaneous	1	2	5
Company's Annual Tea ...	1	2	6
Balance in hand	6	13	10
	£22	2	1

J. F. HAYES, Captain.

ST. GEORGE'S RANGERS AND GUIDES.

Receipts.	£	s.	d.
Balance brought forward ...	8	8	10½
Subscriptions	1	5	4
Hut Charges		8	3
Bank Interest		5	0
	£10	7	5½

Expenditure.	£	s	d.
Room Charges	1	10	0
Hut Charges	2	0	0
Brownies Toadstool	1	10	6
Caretaker		2	6
Badges and Books		8	5
Subscriptions (Miss Yates) ...		2	8½
Uniform on hand		13	0
Balance in hand	4	0	4
	£10	7	5½

Misses D. LOWE and A. BENNETT.

ST. GEORGE'S BROWNIES.

Receipts.	£	s.	d.
Balance brought forward ...	1	14	0
Subscriptions	1	13	1
	£3	7	1

Expenditure.	£	s.	d.
Badges		3	0
Caretaker		2	6
Postages, Books, etc. ...		3	7
Frame for Registration Certificate		2	9
Subscriptions (Miss Yates) ...		2	6
Balance in hand	2	12	9
	£3	7	1

E. COWEN and G. BENNETT.

7

ST. GEORGE'S SUNDAY SCHOOLS ACCOUNT.

RECEIPTS.	£	s.	d.
To Balance in hand	2	5	0
„ Collection at Prize Giving ...	1	6	6
„ Grant from Churchwardens	14	0	0
„ Proceeds of Entertainments (per Rev. N. Panter) ...	3	1	0
„ Profit on Teachers' Social ...	1	8	0
„ Profit on Concert (per Mrs. Watson)	1	0	0
„ Hire of Confirmation Veils (per Miss Knowles) ...		7	2
„ Profit on Dance in Parish Room (per H. Brown) ...		11	0
	£23	18	8

EXPENDITURE.	£	s.	d.
By One Hundred Hymn Books (words only)	2	10	0
„ Three Music Books ...		10	6
„ Registers and Cards ...		10	7
„ Messrs. Cheshire's Account, Prize Books, etc.	8	15	0
„ Girls', Infants', Morning Schools and Hoobrook School Prizes	2	15	0
„ Extra Hymn Books ...		15	6
„ Hospitality to Deanery Teachers	1	0	0
„ Note Books and Pencils ...		2	6
„ Picture Books for Infants		2	8
„ Prizes for Boys' School (W. H. Smith Account) ...	1	7	11
„ Hospitality to Deanery Teachers	1	0	0
„ Subscription to Diocesan Association		5	0
„ Balance in hand	4	4	0
	£23	18	8

Examined and found correct.
REV. J. W. F. BOUGHEY, *Hon. Auditor.* T. R. BADLAND, *Hon. Sec. and Treas.*

WHITSUNTIDE SUNDAY SCHOOLS TREAT ACCOUNT.

RECEIPTS.	£	s.	d.
To Balance in hand (1935) ...	5	4	11
„ Collections in St. George's Church, Whit Sunday ...		7	11
„ Collections in St. George's Church, Whit Monday ...	1	0	0
„ Subscriptions	11	3	4
	£17	16	2

EXPENDITURE.	£	s.	d.
By Cost of Band in Procession	1	13	4
„ Hire of Lorries, etc. ...	3	0	0
„ Prizes	1	7	6
„ Carrying Banner		10	0
„ Erecting Tables, etc. ...		10	0
„ Tea, Cakes, etc.	5	3	0
„ Caretaker of Parish Room and Clearing Playground		10	0
Cutting Grass in Field, etc.		15	0
„ Hire of Bunting and Flags		5	0
„ Balance in hand	4	2	4
	£17	16	2

Examined and found correct.
REV. B. J. ISAAC, *Hon. Auditor.* T. R. BADLAND, *Hon. Sec. and Treas.*

ST. GEORGE'S PARISH MAGAZINE.

Receipts	£	s.	d.
Balance brought forward	2	13	1
Sales during 1936	47	2	10
	£49	15	11

Expenditure	£	s.	d.
Cheshire & Sons	49	13	3
Balance in hand		2	8
	£49	15	11

HAROLD EVERS, Hon. Sec.

ST. GEORGE'S CHURCHYARD FUND.

1936	Receipts.	£	s.	d.
Jan. 1.	To Balance in hand ...	4	11	0
	„ Mrs. Hayward ...		5	0
	„ The Misses Minifie		10	0
	„ Dr. J. C. Griffiths	2	0	0
	„ Mrs. Morgan's Legacy	8	14	8
	„ Mrs. W. Hill		2	6
	„ Mr. A. W Brown ...		2	6
	„ Mrs. Foster		2	6
	„ Miss Coley Power ...		5	0
	„ Mrs. D. Wise		2	6
	„ Mr. T. H. Williams ...		2	6
	„ Mr. J. Findon ...		5	0
	„ Mrs. Hibberd		2	6
	„ Mr. H. Deacon ...		5	0
	„ Mr. F. Ayres		2	6
		£17	13	2

1936	Expenditure.	£	s.	d.
June, July, Aug.	By cutting grass (H. Jordan and F. Brooks six weeks at 35/.) ...	10	10	0
Sept.	„ Weed killer on paths, time and materials ...		18	0
July, Aug. Nov. Dec	„ Flowers for Anniversaries, Holly Wreaths for Xmas, cleaning Stones and cutting grass to comply with Mrs. Morgan's legacy ...	1	10	0
Dec.	„ By putting Grass and Wreath on the grave of Mr. J. Nicholls to comply with legacy ...		10	0
Dec. 31	„ Balance in hand ...	4	5	2
		£17	13	2

Examined and found correct,
T. R. BADLAND, Hon Secretary and Treasurer. J. B. S. ROBINSON.

ST. GEORGE'S FONT FUND.

1936	Receipts.	£	s.	d.
Jan. 1	To Balance in hand ...	11	0	7
Dec. 31	„ Bank interest ...		2	11
		£11	3	6

1936	Expenditure.	£	s.	d.
Nov. 30	By Transferred to Organ Fund	11	3	6
		£11	3	6

Examined and found correct,
H. COOK,
W. G. GETHIN,

C. J. VINEY,
T. R. BADLAND, *Churchwardens.*

ST. GEORGE'S PARISH ROOM FUND.

Receipts.

	£	s.	d.
Balance from 1935	4	11	9
Socials and Parties	5	12	6
Mrs. Pugh's Dancing Class ...	5	12	6
St. George's Mothers' Union ...		12	6
St. George's Burial Club ...	1	5	0
St. George's Rangers	3	0	0
St. George's Girls' Club ...	1	0	0
Proceeds of Rummage Sales ...	4	7	6
	£26	1	9

Expenditure.

		£	s.	d.
Kidderminster Corporation Water Rate			6	0
K. & D.E.L. Co. Ltd. Electric Light, etc.		6	9	3
Austin Bros, Coal		6	0	11
Mrs. Lloyd, Wood				
Allowance ...	... 13 6			
Less Insurance	... 9 6			
			4	0
H. Potter, Sweeping Chimneys and Cleaning Windows ...			16	0
Kidderminster Gas. Co.		1	19	2
Fire Insurance			12	6
National Health Insurance Stamps		2	11	4
Electric Lamps		1	8	9
" Repairs			17	6
Crocks Fund			15	0
Cash in Hand		4	1	4
		£26	1	9

Examined and found correct.
EVERARD E. LAVERS, *Hon. Auditor.* ERIC O. SAVERY, *Hon. Secretary.*

Church Missionary Society—Kidderminster Association.

Receipts.

	£	s.	d.
To Miss Fawcett's Social ...	2	0	0
" Miss Bint—Boxes	6	1	7
" Exhibition Doll's House ...		11	2
" Boys' Brigade	3	10	0
" Subscriptions per Mrs. Wilkins	3	3	0
" American Tea and Lecture	20	0	0
" Missionary Week-end Collections	6	5	0
" Miss Bint—Boxes	4	18	4
" Miss Timmis M.S.L. ...	1	15	0
" Duplex	8	18	2
	£57	2	3

Expenditure.

	£	s.	d.
To Midland Bank, Worcester ...	11	15	9
" Salisbury Square, London ...	3	10	0
" Midland Bank, Worcester ...	35	0	0
" Balance in hand	6	16	6
	£57	2	3

In addition to the above, between six and seven pounds has been collected during the year in the Sunday Schools for the S.P.G. for the support of a girl in India and also for a boy in South America.

A. C. BLENCOWE, *Hon. Treasurer.*

ST. GEORGE'S BURIAL CLUB.

Receipts.

	£	s.	d.
To Balance in hand	53	7	6
" Members' Payments—			
January 3rd	26	12	0
January 31st	28	10	6
February 28th	27	8	0
March 27th Qr.	30	9	0
April 24th	26	18	0
May 22nd	25	17	6
June 19th Qr.	27	1	6
July 17th	27	14	0
August 14th	26	17	0
September 11th Qr. ...	31	15	0
October 9th	28	2	6
November 6th	26	9	6
December 4th Qr. ...	35	7	6
" Interest from Bank ...	1	12	5
" Entrance Fees		15	0
" Sale of Rules			10
	£424	17	9

Expenditure.

	£	s.	d.
By John Thomas Jones ...	5	0	0
" Susannah Mallard	5	0	0
" George Wiltshire	5	0	0
" William Burden	5	0	0
" Winifred Chandler ...	5	0	0
" Elsie May Ellis	5	0	0
" Hannah Clifford	5	0	0
" George Lane	5	0	0
" Charles Jones	5	0	0
" John Dugard	5	0	0
" Louisa Ellen Baynton ...	5	0	0
" George Dando	5	0	0
" Thomas Thatcher	5	0	0
" Eliza Parker	5	0	0
" Alfred John Jones	5	0	0
" Cheshire & Sons Ltd.—New Cards, Balance Sheets and Envelopes	2	6	6
" Hire of Parish Room ...	1	5	0
" Sundries, Stamps, etc. ...		15	6
" Salary of Secretary to December, 1936	10	0	0
" Returned to 377 members ...	257	5	6
" Cash in hand	4	14	0
" Balance in Bank (includes Tea Reserve)	73	11	3
	£424	17	9

Examined and found correct.
EVERARD E. LAVERS, *Hon. Auditor.* Rev. B. J. ISAAC, M.A. *President.*
MARJORY CARTER, *Secretary and Treasurer,* 184, Chester Road North.

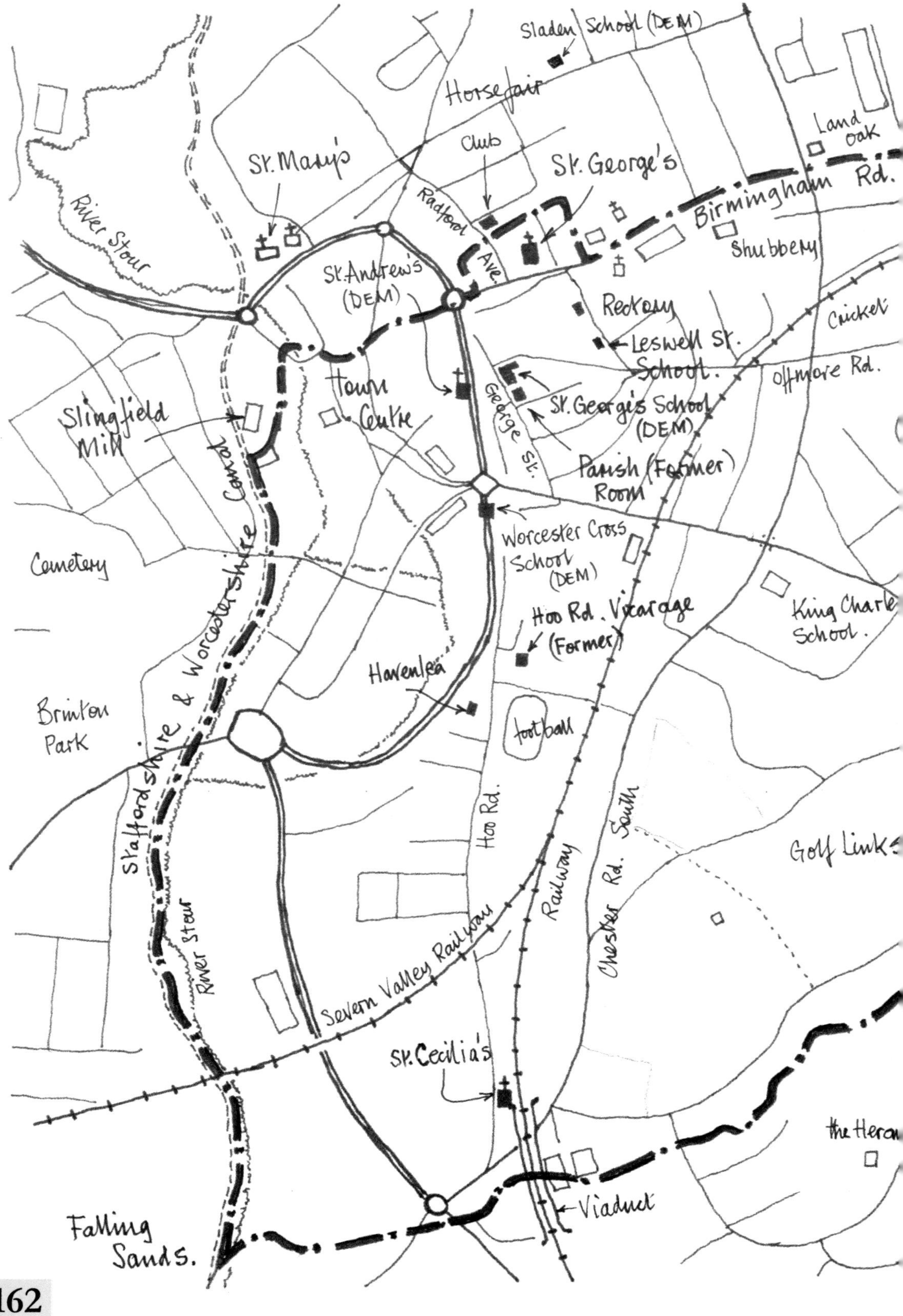

Sladen School (DEM)
Horsefair
Land oak
St. Mary's
Club
St. George's
Birmingham Rd.
River Stour
Radford Ave.
Shrubbery
St. Andrew's (DEM)
Rectory
Leswell St. School.
Cricket
Offmore Rd.
Town Centre
Slingfield Mill
George St.
St. George's School (DEM)
Parish (Former) Room
Worcester Cross School (DEM)
Cemetery
Staffordshire & Worcestershire Canal
King Charles School.
Hoo Rd. Vicarage (Former)
Havenlea
Brinton Park
football
Hoo Rd.
Chester Rd. South
Railway
Golf Links
Severn Valley Railway
River Stour
St. Cecilia's
the Heron
Viaduct
Falling Sands.

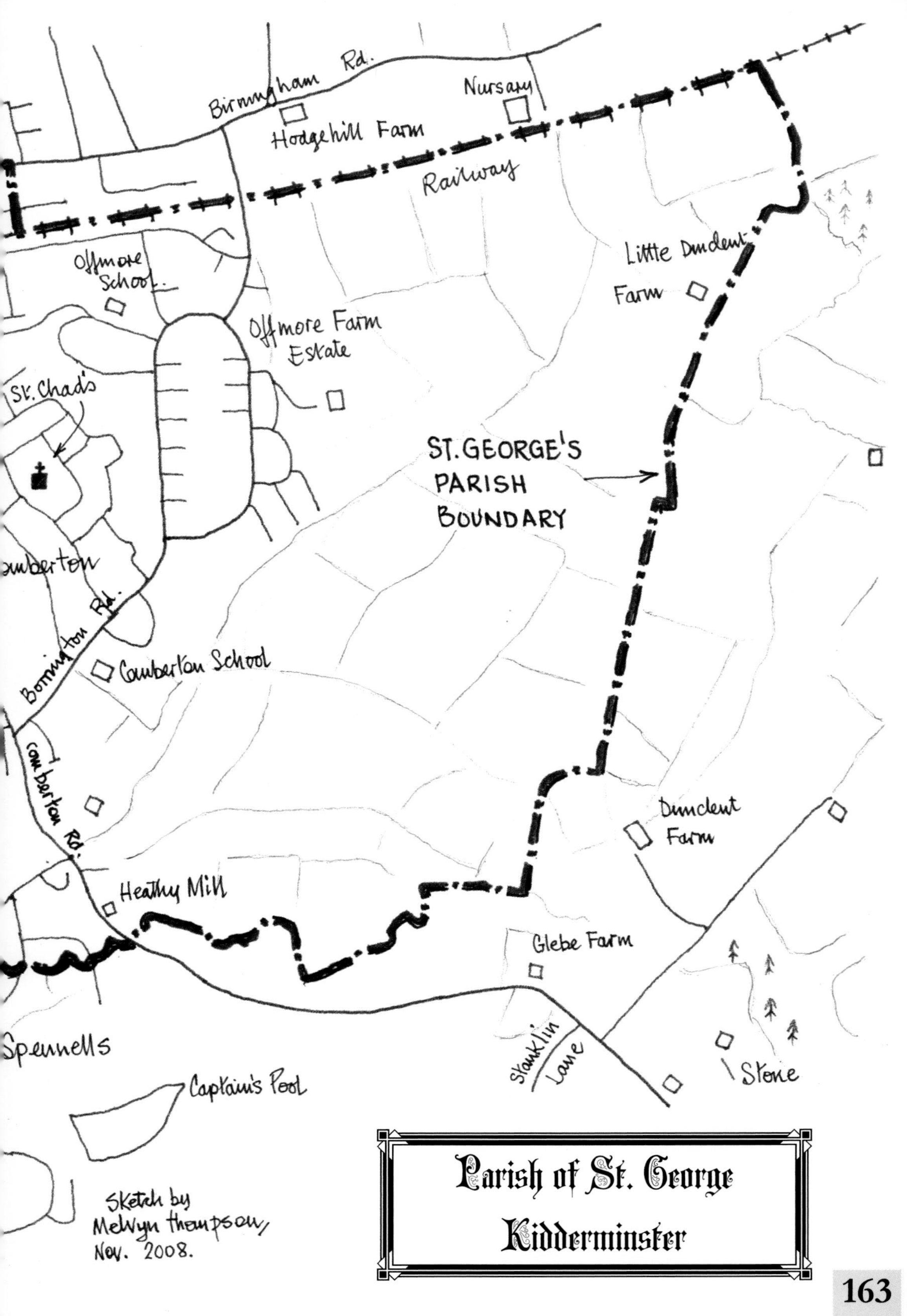
Birmingham Rd.
Nursary
Hodgehill Farm
Railway
Offmore School.
Offmore Farm Estate
St. Chad's
Little Dunclent Farm
ST. GEORGE'S PARISH BOUNDARY
Comberton
Bonnington Rd.
Comberton School
Comberton Rd.
Dunclent Farm
Heathy Mill
Glebe Farm
Spennells
Stanklin Lane
Stone
Captain's Pool
Parish of St. George
Kidderminster
Sketch by Melvyn Thompson, Nov. 2008.

I AM the VINE
You are the branches